EN ROUTE TO THE
GREAT EASTERN CIRCUS

Borgo Press Books by WILLIAM L. SLOUT

Amphitheatres and Circuses: A History from Their Earliest Date to 1861, with Sketches of Some of the Principal Performers, by Col. T. Allston Brown (editor)

Broadway Below the Sidewalk: Concert Saloons of Old New York (editor)

Broadway's Poor Relation: Plays and Players of Repertoire and Stock, 1920-1930

The Burial of Alma: A Comedy in Two Acts

Burnt Cork and Tambourines: A Source Book for Negro Minstrelsy (editor)

Chilly Billy: The Evolution of a Circus Millionaire

Clowns and Cannons: The American Circus During the Civil War

En Route to the Great Eastern Circus and Other Essays on Circus History

From Rags to Ricketts and Other Essays on Circus History

Fun and Fancy in Old New York: Selections from a Series, "Reminiscences of a Man about Town," by Col. Tom Picton (editor)

Grand Entrée: The Birth of the Greatest Show on Earth, 1870-1875 (with Stuart L. Thayer)

Ink from a Circus Press Agent: An Anthology of Circus History from the Pen of Charles H. Day, by Charles H. Day (editor)

Joe Blackburn's A Clown's Log, Second Edition, by Charles H. Day (editor)

Life Upon the Wicked Stage: A Visit to the American Theatre of the 1860s, 1870s, and 1880s As Seen in the Pages of the New York Clipper (editor)

Old Gotham Theatricals: Selections from a Series, "Reminiscences of a Man about Town," by Col. Tom Picton (editor)

Olympians of the Sawdust Circle: A Biographical Dictionary of the Nineteenth-Century American Circus

Popular Amusements in Horse & Buggy America: An Anthology of Contemporaneous Essays (editor)

A Royal Coupling: The Historic Marriage of Barnum and Bailey

Theatre in a Tent: The Development of Provincial Entertainment

The Theatrical Rambles of Mr. and Mrs. John Greene, Second Edition, by Charles Durang (editor)

The Trial of Dr. Jekyll: An Adaptation of Robert Louis Stevenson's "The Strange Case of Dr. Jekyll and Mr. Hyde": A Play in Two Acts

EN ROUTE TO THE GREAT EASTERN CIRCUS

AND OTHER ESSAYS ON CIRCUS HISTORY

WILLIAM L. SLOUT

THE BORGO PRESS
MMXI

Clipper Studies in the Theatre
ISSN 0748-237X

Number Twenty

EN ROUTE TO THE GREAT EASTERN CIRCUS

Copyright © 1995, 1996, 2005, 2006, 2007, 2011 by
William L. Slout

FIRST EDITION

Published by Wildside Press LLC

www.wildsidebooks.com

EN ROUTE TO THE GREAT EASTERN CIRCUS

CONTENTS

ACKNOWLEDGMENTS 9
EN ROUTE TO THE GREAT EASTERN
    CIRCUS 11
THE GREAT EASTERN CIRCUS OF 1872. . . 109
THE NOT-SO-GREAT TRANS-ATLANTIC
    CIRCUS AND MENAGERIE 139
WHAT GOES UP…COMES DOWN 157
THE CHICKEN OR THE EGG?. 179
ABOUT THE AUTHOR 205

ACKNOWLEDGMENTS

These essays have been previously published as follows, and are reprinted (with minor editing, updating, and textual modifications) by permission of the author:

"*En Route* to the Great Eastern Circus," was published in *Bandwagon: The Journal of the Circus Historical Society, Inc.*, Vol. 50, No. 3 (March-April, 2006), p. 28-36; Vol. 50, No. 3 (May-June, 2006), p. 24-33; Vol. 50, No. 4 (July-August, 2006), p. 32-39; Vol. 50, No. 5 (September-October, 2006), p. 17-25. Copyright © 2006, 2011 by William L. Slout.

"The Not-So-Great Trans-Atlantic Circus and Menagerie" was published in *Bandwagon: The Journal of the Circus Historical Society, Inc.*, Vol. 49, No. 6 (November-December, 2005), p. 38-42. Copyright © 2005, 2011 by William L. Slout.

"What Goes Up...Comes Down," was presented at the Circus Historical Society convention in San Antonio, Texas on October 19, 1995, and published in *Bandwagon: The Journal of the Circus Historical Society, Inc.*, Vol. 40, No. 2 (March-April, 1996), p. 22-27. Copyright © 1995, 1996, 2011 by William L. Slout.

"The Chicken or the Egg: A Double Ring Controversy, Phase Two" and published in *Bandwagon: The Journal of the Circus Historical Society, Inc.*, Vol. 51, No. 1 (January-February, 2007), p. 29-36. Copyright © 2007, 2011 by William L. Slout.

"The Great Eastern Circus of 1872: A Fantastical Journey" is published here for the first time. Copyright © 2011 by William L. Slout.

EN ROUTE TO THE GREAT EASTERN CIRCUS

Charles H. Day kindled my interest in the Great Eastern Circus while I was compiling and editing his many writings for *Ink from a Circus Press Agent*. An intriguing comment read quite simply, "The circus ship, *Great Eastern*, was practically launched on wind for lack of capital and sailed to success on a light I.O.U. It was one of the most audacious ventures ever attempted by a management."[1]

The metaphor was inspired by the British *Great Eastern* steamship, launched in 1858. She was larger than anything before it and several years after it. Its celebrity was established in America in 1860 when it made a record-breaking trip from Liverpool to New York City. As it lay in harbor after the crossing, an entrance fee was charged the curious of the city to go aboard and look around.

Exemplifying its popularity, a huge horse, said to have come from Belgium, was named after the ship and exhibited in Boston. The mammoth equine weighed

---

1. Charles H. Day, "Happy Days at the St. Charles," *Billboard*, November 5, 1904. This item was included in *Ink from a Circus Press Agent*. (San Bernardino, CA) The Borgo Press, 1995.

something like 2,300 pounds, with a girth of nine and a half feet, and stood nearly twenty hands high. And although Nixon & Kemp's Great Eastern Circus was the first of that title, it was operating a year before the ship's debut; the "Eastern" actually referred to the section of the country in which the show performed.

The Great Eastern of our narrative was conceived and carried out in 1872 by three very absorbing circus entrepreneurs—George W. DeHaven, Andrew Haight and R. E. J. Miles—whose lives were interwoven in a series of professional ups and downs that make for an interesting chronicle. We will be reporting the circus activities of these three men up to the forming of the Great Eastern, hence the *En Route* in the title.

George W. DeHaven was born in Jackson County, Ohio, March 22, 1837. His mother died when he was very young; so when he became twelve years of age his widowed father, Abraham DeHaven, gave him $200 in gold and told him to shift for himself. His father, then, became his first of many financial backers. With this capital, he purchased a team of oxen and a plow and hired out for farm labor. Later he acquired a threshing machine to work the wheat fields. However, such labor became too menial for a young man of DeHaven's ambition; so in 1858, from the money he had saved, he bought an interest in a circus.[2]

DeHaven was a man who would take out any show as often as he could find a backer for it. With this uncanny ability to talk a circus into being, it is claimed

---

2. W. W. Durand, *Great Eastern Route Book*, 1872.

he organized and put on the road some thirty-three different outfits during his career. "[He is] a hustler of indomitable perseverance, resourceful and relentless, and if any man can organize a show and run it on wind, he can," agent Charley Pell was quoted. "The most successful of men have been laughed at and derided and George W. DeHaven may be in that class, and to prove to you the faith that is in me, I would engage to him tomorrow and take my chances."[3]

Agent W. W. Durand's biographical sketch in the 1872 Great Eastern route book, for a circus of which DeHaven was a co-proprietor, is the original source of DeHaven's activities prior to 1860. Unfortunately, some of what is included has proven unreliable; so it must be treated with some skepticism.

Durand described him as a man of splendid presence who, in his prime, was tall, cool, gray-eyed, broad of forehead, of athletic stature, solid and muscular, and with an active step and speech.

> "Perhaps no other man in the profession has such manifestly excellent qualities to fit him for the position, so responsible, of manager as DeHaven. He has a mysterious command and influence over his army of actors, working men and attaches, that is at once inexplicable and yet effectual. His orders or wishes are ever obeyed, and so quietly, that one would suppose that his men had been trained under the most

---

3. John M. Henderson, "Winning Wealth with Wind," *Billboard*, September 7, 1907.

rigid discipline, which is not the case. He is supreme among his people, and yet one would never suppose it from any word or action of his. DeHaven was by nature intended for a manager, and he does the old Dame credit."

Durand wrote that in 1858 DeHaven "secured the co-operation of the widely-known Oliver Bell, and organized and equipped an excellent arena and equestrian establishment, at Cedarville, Ill., which was closed at Green Bay, Wisconsin, the fall of that year." We know that Bell was co-proprietor of Satterlee, Bell & Co.'s Great American Circus in 1858. The use of "& Co." in the title suggests that Satterlee and Bell were not the only owners; so it is possible that DeHaven was a silent partner. However, the company did not perform at either Cedarville or Green Bay, as we shall see; and, to make things more confusing, DeHaven's name does not appear in any of the Satterlee & Bell newspaper items we have been able to find. It was not included within an advertisement in the Covington *Journal* of April 24, or the Cincinnati *Daily Enquirer* of May 5, or the Toledo *Blade* of May 17, or the Columbia (MO) *Weekly Statesman* of August 13. On the other hand, the fact that DeHaven became a partner of Bell's for the 1860 season implies they had some prior relationship; so let us proceed with the shaky assumption that he was connected in some way with this organization.

R. C. Satterlee had been the manager for Major Brown's Mammoth Colloseum [sic] the previous year and Oliver Bell was the principal rider. Thayer tells us they purchased the Harry Buckley circus, which Buckley had closed with the intention of retiring from the business.

Bell's professional career dated back to at least 1836, connecting with such early organizations as Frost & Co., Bacon & Derious, and Welch & Bartlett. In his youth, while serving his apprenticeship, he was known as Oliver Bacon, in deference to his mentor, Charles Bacon. Agent John Dingess once described his principle act as "among the posies of equestrianism." Therefore, from his twenty-plus years in the circus business, Bell was able to share his wisdom with DeHaven, then a twenty-one-year-old novice.

The opening for Satterlee, Bell & Co. occurred on May 3 and 4 at Covington, Kentucky, just across the Ohio River from Cincinnati where the outfit had been stored. The "array of Star Performers never before equaled" listed in the opening ads consisted of Bell, Thomas Neville, Oliver Worstel, Hiram Marks and Mlle. Louise, riders; John Davenport and Dan Castello, clowns (this is the first reference to Castello we have seen); Charles Morrison, acrobat; I. W. Tucker, contortionist; John Wolfington, juggler; Mlle. Antoinette, ascensionist; and a perch act called the Andalusian Brothers. The performing roster appears to have remained intact at least through mid-August.[4] E. O. Reed was the bandleader, whose aggregation, the ads proclaimed, would be driven through the streets in a

---

4. Advertisements in Covington (KY) *Journal*, April 24, 1858; Cincinnati (OH) *Daily Enquirer*, May 5, 1858; Chicago (IL) *Tribune*, July 2, 1858; Columbia (MO) *Weekly Statesman*, August 13, 1858.

band chariot pulled by thirty-six horses, two abreast. Mlle. Antoinette was purported to be the only lady to make the ascension on a single wire without a balance pole. "Only Company that Performs Everything on the Bills." The admission price was 50¢ for box seats and 25¢ for the pit.[5] One can assume that the cheaper ticket was for standing room.

Conditions were bad in the country at this time, in part caused by the Panic of 1857, thus ending twelve years of prosperity. This was particularly apparent in the industrial states of the North. A political distraction in Illinois, brought about by the senatorial race between Abraham Lincoln and his Democrat opponent, Stephen A. Douglas, included seven debates in all, out of which came the memorable, "A house divided against itself cannot stand."

A number of circuses went to the barn early. It nearly happened to Satterlee, Bell & Co. at Chicago, where the circus had set up at the Water Works lot on Adams Street for the fourth of July weekend, the 2nd, 3rd, and 5th. However, the proprietors managed to survive and finish the tour, which included stands in Ohio, Michigan, Indiana, Illinois, Wisconsin and ending in Carrolton, Missouri, some time past mid-September. This terminated the firm of Satterlee, Bell & Co.

Durand claimed that in the spring of 1859 the show went out, closing in the fall at "Duwardugiac," Michigan. This is erroneous. Facts show that DeHaven & Bell's outfit closed at Dowagiac, Michigan, in 1860.

---

5. *Ibid.*

In 1859, Satterlee went off to manage J. O. Davis & Orlando Crosby's French and American Circus. Oliver Bell joined Hyatt & Co. in Ohio.

Hyatt & Co. was a railroad show—"Wait for the Fast Train! Progressing with the Age! Ahead of the Old Time Exhibitors." Along with Bell, the roster of Frank Hyatt's circus included Frank Stark, John Naylor, Hiram Marks, and Mlle. Victorine, riders; George Archer, globe performer; Nat Rogers, rider and gymnast; T. Williams, strong man; Joe Dickson and Tom Osborn, clowns; Ben Gresh and Eli Burke, trapeze performers; and Mlle. Josephine on the rope. Herr Bunnell's Military Band provided the music. John Dingess was the agent. As with the previous circus described, admissions were 50¢ for boxes, 25¢ for the pit, and half price for children.[6]

Unfortunately, the company lasted only a week before going broke, perhaps closing in Indianapolis on May 17. Shortly, a new organization was formed there by Nat Rogers and George Archer, known as the Great Railroad Circus. We learn from John Glenroy, who joined in July, that this outfit was comprised of members of the defunct Hyatt group—Oliver Bell, William Sparks, Gresh & Burke, and Mlle. Victorine. Added to them were William Donovan, gymnast and Lee Powell and Charles Brown, clowns. Glenroy recalled that from the outset the show was in deep trouble, forcing the sheriff to intervene. "On arriving in Indianapolis, I found the whole concern in the hands

---

6. Richmond (IN) *Palladium*, May 5, 1859.

of the sheriff, and everything in such a fearful condition that no one seemed to know what to do," Glenroy wrote. "The performers were so badly off that the sheriff, as an act of charity, allowed them to give two performances on the fourth of July—one in the afternoon and the other in the evening."[7]

This last chance was moderately successful. It allowed the company to continue operating until July 12, when a man named McCorkle stepped in and took over the reins. He guided the company on a brief tour through Indiana and then into Chicago for a week, where, unfortunately, at the end of the stand he disappeared with whatever cash there was. The stranded actors were saved for a time by a showman-turned-Chicago-hotel-keeper, Abner Pell, who leased the outfit for a week to perform during the fair season at Freeport, Illinois. The circus equipment was then returned to Chicago where it was sold through the office of the sheriff.[8]

With Satterlee and Bell both gone, what became of DeHaven? The touring scheme under the Great Union Circus title, which Durand erroneously referred to as beginning at Cedarville, Illinois, and traveling as far north as Green Bay, Wisconsin, occurred in 1860 with Bell and DeHaven possibly acquiring the Satterlee & Bell tent and equipment. But nothing has been found of DeHaven's whereabouts for the circus season of 1859.

We know DeHaven was teamed with Bell in 1860 in

---

7. Glenroy, John H. *Ins and Outs of Circus Life*. Boston: M. M. Wing & Co., 1885, pp. 116-118.

8. *Ibid.*

organizing a railroad show under the patriotic title of Great Union Circus. John Glenroy joined at Dubuque, Iowa, in July as a rider. In his book of reminiscences he recalled the performers as being Bell, rider and acrobat; Charlie Brown, clown and acrobat; William Sparks, cannon ball performer; Tom Burgess, clown; Henry Morrast and Fred Spreckel, gymnasts; P. H. Seaman, clown and minstrel; and Annie Seaman, dancer. An advertisement in the Dubuque *Herald* at this time listed Bell, DeHaven, Burgess, Morrast, and Brown. Added were Fred Warner, Samuel Day, Charles Huntington and Mlle. Louise, with no mention of the Seamans.[9] The Freeport *Bulletin* advertisement in May listed Bell, Marks, Sparks, Morrast, Burgess, Mlle. Louise, Charles Huntington, the Ellsler Brothers, and Herr Kline.[10] This illustrates how flexible and even unreliable company rosters could be in the course of a season, as performers came and went and as proprietors used names in a somewhat careless manner. Unfortunately, this adds confusion to one's narrative.

By August the following artists were advertised: Bell, Sparks, Brown, Glenroy, Morrast, Burgess, Seaman, Huntington, Herr Kline, Charley Clark, and Fred Warner. We cannot explain Herr Kline, but we do know he was not Herr Andre Kline, the famous tightrope dancer. A Miss Azlene Allen was also included as a "modest and most charming equestrienne and *danseuse*." There was a concert or after-show offered

---

9. Dubuque (IA) *Herald*, July 11, 1860.

10. Freeport (IL) *Bulletin*, May 3, 1860.

after each performance by the New Orleans Serenaders for the admission of 20¢. There was also, what was described as a "Splendid Band Cavalcade," Nye's Excelsior Brass Band, mounted on caparisoned horses, used to ballyhoo the streets.[11]

DeHaven & Co. opened the 1860 tour in Cedarville, Illinois, on the 1st of May. The show then worked its way north through Iowa and arrived at St. Paul, Minnesota, by steamboat. The June 6 performance there was marred by the collapse of a section of bleachers, resulting in some broken bones. DeHaven reacted to the accident with an explanation in the *Daily Pioneer*:

> "The proprietors of the Circus wish to state that they are convinced that the accident was occasioned by the rascality of someone interfering with the stands upon which the seats are placed, and that they have made the most liberal offers in behalf of those who were injured through no fault of their own...."[12]

The item did not satisfy the victims, who unhesitatingly filed claims for damages. A sheriff's deputy was assigned to accompany the circus out of town to safeguard the physical assets while legal proceedings determined liability. The *Daily Pioneer* reported that the "lawyers and the sheriff stuck to them like chestnut burs to the last."

---

11. Aurora (IL) *Beacon*, August 16, 1860.

12. Loeffler, Part 1, p. 28, quoting the St. Paul (MN) *Pioneer and Democrat*, June 9, 1860.

In leaving, the outfit was loaded onto a boat and moved along the Minnesota as far as Mankato, where the river makes a sharp curve northward, and continued on to Redwood Falls and the Lower Sioux Agency. There the circus performed for an audience made up chiefly of Indians. The Mankato *Weekly Record* portrayed the occasion with:

> "DeHaven's circus visited the Lower Sioux Agency last week, and was patronized by crowded houses of delighted Indians. The first exhibition was given the day before payment, and we are told the Indians were willing to trade blankets, guns, and almost any article they possessed for tickets or admission. The tent was crowded, in consequence of which many were denied admission. When anything occurred eliciting their admiration, those on the inside shouted, which was responded to by those on the outside. Many white persons attended the exhibitions merely to witness the actions of the Indians, which, we are told, were more novel and interesting than the feats of the performers."[13]

The boat and its party made their way back again to St. Paul, exhibiting there on June 29 and 30. A benefit performance was presented on the latter date.

---

13. *Ibid.*, p. 29, quoting the *Mankato Weekly Record*, June 26, 1860.

> "DeHaven's Circus Company proposes to give a grand exhibit this afternoon, June 30th, commencing at 2 o'clock for the benefit of Miss Lillie Collins, one of [the] parties injured by the falling of the seats at one of the performances recently in this city. The proprietors assure us that every effort will be made to give general satisfaction."[14]

The company had moved back into Iowa by July. During a performance at Dubuque on the 12th Bell's act of jumping through a hoop surrounded by a dozen knives ran into trouble. For whatever reason, his classic leap went awry and he was impaled by the sharp objects. He quickly tended to his wounds, remounted and performed the leap again to success. One of the novelties of DeHaven's program was an equestrian act called "Mother Goose, or, The Man Who Lost His Wife." It is an old subject, a *Clipper* correspondent confirmed, "but, nevertheless, with new handling, may prove very entertaining."[15]

Not entertaining enough apparently, for the money ran out in late July at Lena, Illinois, forcing the show to lay over until a backer could be found. Glenroy wrote, "At the end of two weeks from the time I joined DeHaven (he was wrong on the timing), he ran short of funds, and we were forced to remain in Lena until

---

14. *Ibid*, p. 29, quoting the St. Paul (MN) *Pioneer and Democrat*, June 30, 1860.

15. New York *Clipper*, September 1, 1860.

cash came to the treasury."[16] And, indeed, it did, from a man by the name of Sam Weaver (Glenroy erroneously called him Sam Matthews).

At this time rail travel was abandoned for touring the country towns until October 5, when again the treasury was depleted and the company was forced to fold at Dowagiac, Michigan. Poor Weaver lost his shirt and the outfit was attached by the sheriff for the back pay owed the performers.[17] This was just one of many DeHaven ventures that would go aground.

It must be that Sam Weaver had more than one shirt, however, because he opened an interim circus at Freeport, Illinois, within a structure he created for such performances. Items in the Freeport *Bulletin* during the tenure of the winter circus do not include DeHaven's name. Only Weaver was referred to as being in charge of the company.

The Freeport *Bulletin* recorded the winter circus activities almost weekly. The troupe was welcomed by the paper on December 20 with:

> "The time for amusements has come, and with it the Union Circus arrived. A grand opening will take place on Christmas day, afternoon at 2 o'clock, and evening at 7 o'clock, at the new building just erected for the purpose, near the Ohio House, on Exchange street. Some of the best performers in the United States have been engaged. Tickets 25 cents."

---

16. Glenroy, p. 119.

17. *Ibid.*, p. 120.

A riding school for ladies and children was also announced to be held in the circus structure with Oliver Bell serving as riding master.

We learn from Glenroy, who was with the company, that there were two performances a week, Saturday afternoons and evenings. The performers were to receive board, lodging and washing, a small amount of money for necessities, and one clear benefit during the season. The corps consisted of about a half-dozen of the summer troupe and a few others including clown and rider and double-somersaulter Henry Gardner, also known as old Buck Gardner, who, as the New York *Clipper* phrased it, had "bid adieu to old 'Bourbon county'" and was himself again.

The Christmas opening must have been a present wrapped in ribbons for most or all of the troupe, for presumably they had been out of a job since the unfortunate August closure. Add to this the reception accorded them in a *Bulletin* item of the 27th:

> "The gathering was large and the performance was good—better than anything of the kind that has been in Freeport for a long time. Mr. Oliver Bell accomplished some feats that we thought was not in the power of any actor to do."

The next performances, equally crowded and equally successful, were presented on New Years Day, according to the *Bulletin* of January 3.

"The company is now thoroughly organized, and is equal to anything of the kind that has ever exhibited in Freeport. The performers can't be excelled anywhere. If men in other occupations would fill their posts as well as the actors in the Union Circus do, there would be less cause for complaint, and much more good would be accomplished." The paper was generous in its admiration of Oliver Bell: "Mr. Bell performs a feat that we have never seen done by any other equestrian. He leaps from a horse under full speed, through a hoop surrounded by steel daggers, several inches long, and very sharp. The act is a frightful one, and requires a skillful performer."

The troupe having no female rider, one was invented in John Glenroy. This was inspired by the notoriety that had been created the previous January at Niblo's Garden in New York City when Omar Kingsley, under the billing of Ella Zoyara, donned female garb nightly in a ruse that fooled everyone but the New York press; yet not before many in the male section of the theatre had sent the boy bouquets and tender notes and other expressions of adoration. Glenroy was billed as the French equestrienne, Mlle. Reine. The masquerade apparently worked in rural Illinois, with no one but company members aware of it. Glenroy claimed it was a nightly occurrence for him to receive flowers and love notes from admiring males, and for the young bucks to hang about the dressing room door in hopes of an introduction to the "French beauty."[18]

The January 9 performance was a benefit for the sufferers in Kansas, which amounted to eighty-two dollars. The *Bulletin* of January 17 offered a "thank you" to the equestrian troupe and the Union Cornet band for their generous services. "If the church, the temperance society, and benevolent enterprises generally, receive aid without asking its donors in what way they made their money, we cannot see why the sufferers in Kansas may not do the same."

On February 7 the public was informed of a "grand performance" for the following Saturday which introduced a new piece, a play appealing to the spirit of the times entitled *Secession; or, The South Carolina Army on a War Footing*. And the *Bulletin* notice added: "... which of itself will be well worth the price of admission." Indeed, seeing a military extravaganza enacted by this small band of equestrians with an even smaller budget must have been quite an experience for the locals.

The performers' benefits began toward the end of February. Oliver Bell's, on the 23rd, included a foot race for a silver goblet. The distance was set at one-quarter of a mile, or eleven laps around the ring. "Those wishing to compete for this prize can leave their names with Mr. Smith, at Prescott's Saloon." In addition, there was a race for $50 between performers Tom Burgess and Buck Gardner.

---

18 *Ibid.*, p. 122.

Mr. and Mrs. P. H. Seaman were next on March 2. The announcement read: "On this occasion more fun novelties, dances, speeches, songs, &c., will be produced than ever before offered at any performances." Among these was a play, *Peter Hontz Family*, in which Seaman used six different voices. Another piece was called *Moze and Lize*. In the same issue of the *Bulletin* it was noted that Madame Seaman was giving dancing lessons at the Keystone Ball Room. "Any person wishing to take lessons in this healthy exercise will call there soon."

The *Bulletin* follow-up on the benefit stated: "The performance was the most amusing given this season. Seaman *always* performs well, but he excelled himself on this occasion. Mrs. S., a perfect character in all she undertakes, received great applause. She never looked or performed better. The house was well filled, and must have yielded a very profitable benefit."

Hiram Marks was recognized on March 9. At this performance a pig with a greased tail was tossed into the arena, with a challenge that any boy who could carry it away by the tail could have it. "There is fun in the bill, and it is no use to have the blues when you can get rid of them for a quarter." For Tom Burgess' benefit on March 23 there was a balloon ascension before the program. It was scheduled for 7:00 P.M. in the circus yard. "Everybody is invited to witness the ascension, whether they visit the Circus or not."

On what was to be the final two performances of the season, Saturday, March 30, proprietor Samuel

Weaver received a complimentary benefit from the entire company. An outstanding feature for this event was the well-traveled Campbell Minstrels, appearing "in their songs, dances, burlesques, &c." The *Bulletin* added: "Mr. Weaver requests us to return his sincere thanks to the citizens of Freeport and surrounding country, who have lent him their liberal support the past winter."

But there is more. In a final gesture of appreciation: "Mr. Weaver, the proprietor of the Union Circus, having tendered to the company the free use of the horses and building, they propose to give another performance to-morrow (Friday) evening, which is positively to be the last of the season." With this, the winter stand closed on the 5th of April, after which the company departed for a summer tour with the Great Union Circus.

The clown, Pete Conklin, has written that he was on the *Floating Palace* showing in New Orleans in 1861 when the Confederates seized the boat and ordered all northern people to leave the South. The performers organized a company under the commonwealth plan, chartered a small steamboat, and "fought and showed" their way up the river, finding it necessary to exhibit under two flags. While making stands along the route from New Orleans to Cincinnati, the circus ran up the Stars and Stripes and the band played "Yankee Doodle" for towns on one side of the river and flew the Palmetto Flag and played "Dixie" for towns on the other side.[19]

---

19. Pete Conklin, Barnum & Bailey annual route book, 1906.

The pertinence of his recollection is that the company was called Dan Castello's Great Show, George H. DeHaven, manager. Unfortunately, it is the sole source of reference about the existence of this circus; and, as we are all aware, reminiscences are often unreliable.

We know that DeHaven was out with his Great Union Circus into August of 1860, but apparently was not a part of the Freeport winter circus that followed. DeHaven's company started again in the spring of 1861, presumably on May 18, only a month after Fort Sumter was fired upon. Going down river at the outset of hostilities to manage the commonwealth company and working his way back up again for the May opening creates a mystifying time span. The confiscation of the *Floating Palace* by Southern authorities has drawn occasional attention from circus historians; but no one has been able come up with a proper source in determining with certainty the date during which it occurred or the circumstances surrounding it.

Let us assume Pete Conklin's recollections are correct. In December of 1860 Spalding and Rogers, proprietors of the *Floating Palace,* leased the tow boat, *James Raymond,* to Dan Rice for his tour upriver to Wisconsin, leaving the *Floating Palace* powerless. When Spalding and Rogers finished a summer tour using their other boat, *Banjo,* they established a winter season in New York at the Old Bowery beginning on November 5, 1860. Dan Castello, recently returned from England, was a member of the company. After the run faded at the end of January, some of the performers were sent to New Orleans to begin a season on the *Floating Palace*. Dan Castello was one of them. Meanwhile, the Campbell's Minstrels, including Pete Conklin, also joined the *Palace* roster. That would put the two men at the site in early 1861, at a time when DeHaven was available to join them. Louisiana seceded from the Union on January 26, which solidified the winds of resentment against all Northerners. It is quite possible that some time following this change of authority the boat was confiscated and the troupe was run off. Another boat was chartered and the commonwealth company was formed.

For the 1861 summer tour of the Great Union, Andrews & Carpenter were the proprietors. DeHaven was the manager, Bell the equestrian director, and Hiram Marks the ringmaster. The agents were D. H. Straight and George R. Bates. The plan was to travel to places along the Illinois Railroad line. Advertising took advantage of northern patriotism with a claim of possessing "the most thoroughly bred Anglo-Saxon horses in the world...not old, worn out, fancy-marked horses of foreign blood, but they are young, fresh, and of pure American stock." It also made use of a more familiar circus name with the claim that the show was a continuation of the late Buckley & Mabie's Great National Circus.

William Sparks was back, as was Hank Gardner, "the regular 'Old Spotty' Merriman, the oldest Clown now living." Add Tom Burgess, the Holland family, Robert Lindley, and Herr von Driesden (an unfamiliar name and may have been an imaginative addition of the ad writer). Music was supplied by Glinn's Silver Bugle Band. For all this the company charged 25¢ to sit in any part of the tent—"all box and no pit," meaning no standing room. DeHaven still did not carry a street procession, although there is reference to a band chariot pulled by ten horses that daily serenaded the townspeople. An ad sarcastically claimed it was "built in the present century, and has never been used by *Nero*, or any of the ancient heroes."

Because the war was heating up, the circus was confined to the safer northern states. Kansas and Missouri, where the slavery issue was being violently contested, were out of the question. Show people were moving out of dangerous locales at a rapid pace and those stuck behind faced a troubling fate. A letter from a performer in Kansas, read,

> "How long we may stay here is very uncertain; for it is certain we may be at any moment attacked by Missouri rebels. The man who comes out west now is a lunatic.... When I shall be able to get away without risking my life, God only knows."[20]

The show was in Wisconsin and Minnesota for much of the summer tour. It left Wisconsin after a July 7 date in Lacrosse for a number of Minnesota towns. We learn from the Rochester *City Post*, in regard to a July 10 visit, that the circus carried forty horses and

---

20. New York *Clipper*, October 26, 1861.

fifty people (this may well have been an exaggeration), including Oliver Bell, the Holland family, Hiram Marks, William Sparks, Madame August, Bob Lindley and Master John. Buck Gardner and Tom Burgess were also mentioned in advertising. The bandwagon pulled by ten horses transported Prof. A. B. Cline and his Great Union Bugle Band around the streets to announce the show's arrival.[21]

Performances at Stillwater on the 19th prompted the *Messenger* to respond with:

> "DeHaven's Circus exhibited in this city on Friday afternoon and evening to very fair business.... Some of the performers were good—some indifferent—others decidedly cheap. It cost only a quarter, however, and perhaps the crowd got the worth of their money."

Thanks to that 25¢ admission, which caused the country people to flock in, the summer business was doing better than expected. R. Sands' circus was in the area at this time, charging 50¢.[22]

The Great Union Circus arrived at St. Paul for performances on Saturday and Monday, July 20 and 22. An advertisement at this time in the *Pioneer and Democrat* reminded the public that the organization was the former "H. Buckley & Mabie's Great National Circus"—two shows combined. The management

---

21. Loeffler, Part 2, p. 27, *The White Tops*, quoting the Rochester (MN) *City Post*, July 10, 1861.

22. Loeffler, Part 2, p. 28.

offered a $1,000 challenge to any company in the country that could compete with its band or its performance. Oliver Bell leaped through his hoop of steel daggers; William Sparks caught his cannon balls; John Holland juggled his two sons about in what has come to be known as a Risley act; Herr von Driesden, a person totally unfamiliar to us, contorted; Johnny Holland juggled balls, cups, knives and was a youthful balancer on the globe; Master Georgie Holland participated in a two-horse feat with Hiram Marks, called the "Greek Slave," apparently a carrying act; Robert Lindley sang comic songs; clowns Tom Burgess and Buck Gardner did their part to enliven the program. Others listed in the ads were: Charley West, E. F. Demming, Lyman Snytchen, Abe Fanekan, Old Kilsey, Joe Brown, La Petite Harmon, Madame Augusta, and "the world renowned drum major," Isaac La Rue, all "un-renowned" to this writer. The public was cautioned that it would be their last chance to hear Glinn's Silver Bugle Band, since they were to be "joining forces under the 'Glorious Stars and Stripes'."

Andrews & Carpenter were listed as proprietors, DeHaven as manager, Bell as equestrian director, Marks as master of the arena, and George R. Bates as general agent.[23] The St. Paul appearances prompted the *Pioneer and Democrat* to report large audiences, with no one leaving the tent dissatisfied. After dates at St. Anthony and Minneapolis, the show returned on the 25th, at which time one of the performances

---

23. Advertisement, St. Paul (MN) *Pioneer and Democrat*, July 19, 1861.

was devoted to the benefit of the hospital fund for Minnesota's First Regiment.

The Great Union was in Wisconsin in August, and then may have finished the season in Illinois. W. W. Durand wrote that dissension arose among the partners "regarding route, conduct of show, etc.," which forced the circus to close at Lena. We have found no evidence to confirm this. However, we learn from Loeffler that at season's end DeHaven went indoors for a winter run at St. Paul, first in a building called the Athenaeum, with a performance on October 31. The next exhibition, for some reason, did not occur until November 20, from which the *Pioneer and Democrat* expressed pleasure the following day. "The burlesque opera is the best we have seen in the city. The gymnastic exhibitions are fully as good as any of the Circus exhibitions."[24]

In December, the company moved to another site. DeHaven had "leased and fitted up at considerable expense, a spacious stone building on Seventh Street, near the International Hotel, as an amphitheatre, and proposes to make it a permanent place of amusement."[25] An advertisement promised performances for each Wednesday and Saturday evenings. An item for December 28 announced that "additional performers of notoriety" had arrived and that the farces *Loan of a Lover* and *Cobbler's Frolic* were being presented. The press prefaced a performance on New Year's night with a suggestion that everyone should dress warmly

---

24. Loeffler, Part 2, p. 29, quoting the St. Paul (MN) *Pioneer and Democrat*, December 19, 1861.

25. *Ibid.*

and followed the next day with: "Notwithstanding the difficulties attending the performance on New Year night, we have heard universal satisfaction."[26] Activity continued at this site into February.

DeHaven left winter quarters with a much stronger cast of notable performers for the 1862 season. This included Louise and Theodore Tourniaire, Burnell Runnells, William Worrell, George Batcheller and William Dutton. DeHaven was listed as proprietor; Samuel Weaver, the money man, was treasurer; Robert Johnson, the ringmaster; John Free, band leader; and Charles F. Lord, agent.[27] Again, the show traveled chiefly in Wisconsin, Iowa and Illinois. Advertisements audaciously boasted of the best riders, superior tumblers, three clowns, and three equestriennes, "and in fact the greatest combination of talented and salaried performers ever congregated under one pavilion."[28] In Iowa the Independence *Civilian* announced the shows arrival with: "The troupe will perform on the 24th inst.; and judging by notices in our State exchanges, we have no hesitancy in saying that the best of satisfaction will be given to those who attend."[29]

The large, expensive roster was too much to handle for a 25¢ company. DeHaven was forced to reorga-

---

26. *Ibid, Pioneer and Democrat*, January 2, 1862.

27. St. Louis (MO) *Republican*, August 18, 1862. Others listed were Henry North, Kate Bailey, Jennie Day, Laurie Hazen, Julia Fitzgerald, P. H. Seaman, Master Charles Seaman, Sam Rinehart, Carr & Burdeau, Gustave Wagstay, John Wilson, and Mons. Fraker.

28. McGregor (IA) *North Iowa Times*, July 15, 1862.

29. Independence (IA) *Civilian*, July 15, 1862.

nize at St. Louis in mid-August with a major turn-over of personnel, removing the highest on the salary list. A September ad carried the names of Hiram Marks, Dan Castello, Joseph Tinkham, Carlo, W. J. Smith, the Holland family, the Conrad brothers and Robert Johnson.[30] Gone were the Tourniaires, Runnells, Worrell, Batcheller, and Dutton.

The change does not seem to have diminished audience appeal. Well, seemingly not. The Quincy, Illinois, *Daily Herald*, hailed the one-day stand with:

> "The performances of DeHaven's Circus in this city on Saturday afternoon and night added to the reputation the company had already acquired as the best that has visited the West for several years…. DeHaven's Circus is not only no humbug, but it is in reality far superior to all that is claimed for it."

The paper expressed appreciation for the company's policy of giving ten percent of the receipts for the benefit of sick and wounded soldiers.[31]

The troupe moved by boat along the rivers, performing in Wisconsin, Iowa and Illinois, until the Great Union Circus reportedly folded in October at Polo, Illinois, an event that probably lost Sam Weaver his final shirt.

Castello ventured into circus proprietorship for the

---

30. Ad book, Circus World Museum, for Keokuk (IA), September 17 and 18.

31. Quincy (IL) *Daily Herald*, September 15, 1862.

first time in 1863. With Matthew VanVleck he put together a wagon show out of Fairplay, Wisconsin—Castello & VanVleck's Mammoth Circus. Richard VanVolkenburg was the manager; Tom Poland, master of the arena; and J. R. Murphy and L. VanVleck were ahead of the show. Castello's trick horse, Monitor, and his educated bull, Don Juan, were featured.[32]

After opening in Dubuque, the tour took the circus through territory in Iowa, Wisconsin, Illinois and Minnesota. In a return to Iowa in September, a late arrival at Keokuk necessitated the canceling of the matinee. The *Daily Gate City* reported that the performances were well attended and applauded their entertainment value. "The Wonderful educated horse, Monitor, manifested a wonderful degree of intelligence, seeming to understand every command and motion of his master. The trained bull, Don Juan, was a new feature in the ring performance and performed excellently."[33] Glenroy was with the show, riding both his somersault and two-horse act. He recalled this being one of the most successful tours he had ever had.

In October the company, which had been traveling by boat along the Ohio River, announced plans to reorganize in St. Louis for a tour of the South. This resulted in changing owners, the new ones being Matthew

---

32. Among the company were William Smith, two-horse rider; John Glenroy, somersault rider; Joseph Tinkham, hurdle rider; Charles Burrows, Richard Hammon, John Burns, and George M. Kelley, acrobats; Natt McCollum, banjoist and Ethiopian entertainer; and Frances Castello (probably Mrs. Dan Castello), rider. Castello and Tom Burgess were the clowns. Glenroy, p. 130.

33. Keokuk (IA) *The Daily Gate City*, September 21, 1863.

VanVleck, Ben Maginley and George W. DeHaven.

Maginley, soon to become a familiar figure in this narrative, was a roly-poly actor who had performed in the major theatres of his time. At the start of the war he was stage manager and low comedian with the Memphis theatre company. Very popular with local audiences, he took a farewell benefit on July 28. However, earlier in the month he had launched his own circus company, which first performed in Illinois towns and then returned to Memphis and into a newly erected wooden amphitheatre suitable for performances of horse dramas. This thirty-one-year-old robust actor, weighing some 240 pounds, entered the arena as a clown for the first time on August 17.

Maginley's company opened in Memphis on August 8 to a most friendly reception, as expressed by the *Daily Bulletin*.

> "Mr. B. R. Maginley, the indomitable, has got up a new attraction, in the shape of a circus, which is at present all the go, and we can't see why it should not be, for if anything can be made to succeed, Maginley can make it. 'Many thousands got in, and yet there were many thousands who tried and couldn't,' as we heard a disappointed gentleman say, who tried, but couldn't."[34]

It was this organization that combined with the VanVleck and DeHaven people to travel as Maginley &

---

34. Memphis (TN) *Daily Bulletin*, August 11, 1863.

VanVleck's Cosmopolitan Circus, with DeHaven assuming the management. At this point Glenroy, still carrying resentment from the 1860 DeHaven debacle, turned in his notice. "I left," he wrote, "as I did not wish to travel in any company that DeHaven was interested in."[35] Dan Castello departed more diplomatically, "returning home to break horses for the next summer."

The first engagement of the new management team was in St. Louis beginning October 7. The circus played to good business, which prompted an announcement to remain for another week. The route ultimately led back to Memphis for October 29 through 31. It was then consolidated with Maginley's Cosmopolitan Circus for a winter season in the Memphis wooden amphitheatre.

Somewhere along the route, DeHaven disappeared, but the circus remained active. At mid-December the *Clipper* announced that "Maginley & VanVleck's Circus [continued] to hold forth at Memphis together with Henry Cooke's troupe of Trained Dogs and Monkeys, and [was] playing to crowded houses."[36]

We learn from Durand that in 1864 DeHaven went out in connection with Dan Castello's Great American Circus. The names of Moore and Gruber were mentioned, probably as the backers. A *Clipper* item listed the title of the company as "DeHaven &

---

35. Glenroy, p. 132.

36. New York *Clipper*, December 19, 1863. To complete his move into the world of the circus, Ben Maginley married Marie Carroll, adopted daughter of two-horse rider W. B. "Barney" Carroll and equestrienne Mary Ann Carroll, at Memphis early in 1864.

Castello."[37] Yet, DeHaven did not serve as manager; that position was filled by Levi J. North, and later by L. B. Lent. At different times the general agent was Gil Eaton and Abner Pell. So, this leaves DeHaven's connection with the Castello circus a mystery.

Castello started from St. Paul with a May 9-11 stand. Then, traveling on the *Jeannette Roberts,* the show went down the Mississippi, stopping at such places as Hastings, Minnesota; Lacrosse, Wisconsin; McGregor, Dubuque, Davenport, and Keokuk, Iowa, and Cairo, Illinois. He then moved up the Ohio River to Shawneetown, still in Illinois; New Albany, and Louisville, Kentucky; then up the Wabash to Vincennes and Terre Haute, Indiana; ending at Chicago in early September. The following month the show was back down the Mississippi and into the White and Arkansas Rivers before connecting with the 17th Corps at Little Rock, under the command of General Steele. This is suggested by a Syracuse *Standard* interview: "In 1864 Mr. Castello organized a circus of his own and started south, and was the first to cross the line of war." It stated he had twelve horses and enough good performers to make out the company. The troupe followed the Seventeenth corps, which was under Steele's command at Little Rock, and gave shows in the camp. Helena, Ball's Bluffs, Pine Bluffs, Vicksburg and other places were visited, and by war's end, Castello was with the troops at Randallsville. He then pushed on to Nashville, spent the summer in

---

37. Durand, Great Eastern route book, 1872; New York *Clipper,* March 26, 1864.

Tennessee and wintered in Kentucky.[38]

The tour was not without danger. The performers had a scare while at Commerce, Missouri. After playing to a good house in the afternoon, there came rumors of rebel guerrillas in the area. With the evening house well filled, the rumors were confirmed by the sight of three rockets being fired into the air from different locations around the town, which created a panic within the troupe. The program was conducted with dispatch, the tent was taken down in record time, and the entire troupe boarded onto their boat, which steamed up the river as fast as the old boilers would allow.[39]

Durand stated that DeHaven ended up in Memphis. This stand was opened on October 3, with plans for a week's stay. "Dan Castello's mammoth tent was again crowded to excess last evening by the admirers of quaint, original humor, ground and lofty tumbling, feats of strength and daring, fine horses, splendid horsemanship, and the tinsel and glitter of the equestrian ring," so read the Memphis *Daily Bulletin* of October 6.

The visit was expanded through Saturday the 15th because of the large turnouts. The *Bulletin* of the 9th revealed:

---

38. Loeffler, Part 4, quoted the St. Paul (MN) *Pioneer and Democrat*, March 31, 1864, identifying the show as being the Castello and DeHaven circus. It may be that DeHaven's name was used at this time because of his popularity in the St. Paul area.

39. Clipping from the Syracuse (NY) *Standard*, 1899. *Jeannette Roberts*, under Capt. F. Aymond, 111 tons, ran the St. Paul-Minnesota River; her earliest is date is 1857, and she was dismantled in 1870.

"By general request and induced by the flattering patronage extended by our citizens, Mr. Dan Castello has concluded to remain in Memphis a few days longer, with his mammoth show. New features will be introduced at each performance, and those who have visited his tent, as well as those who have not, will find an entirely new and interesting programme."

A group of citizens encouraged a benefit for Castello. In an item to the *Daily Bulletin* of the 12th, the invitation read:

"A number of your friends and admirers, have, with pleasure, witnessed your plan of conducting an Equestrian Establishment, both in the departments of business and art, [and] feel it incumbent upon them to tender to you some mark of open appreciation. A complimentary benefit and celebration, in which all your well-wishers can participate, has been proposed, to be observed at any time best adapted to your convenience."[40]

This was signed by a number of prominent people of Memphis. Such a message leaves no doubt as to who was the proprietor of the circus.

The performance, which occurred on the 14th, appears to have been a success, according to the *Bulletin* of the 15th:

---

40. New York *Clipper*, July 16, 1864.

> "The marquee of Dan Castello was crowded to its utmost capacity last evening by his numerous friends and admirers, and the popular *beneficiare*, at the close of the entertainment found himself the recipient of a very flattering testimonial of the public's appreciation of the prince of humorists."

Then, according to Durand, before leaving Memphis DeHaven organized a minstrel troupe for the winter, which worked its way north as far as Beaver Dam, Wisconsin. It was there that Andrew Haight comes into our story; when, in 1865, DeHaven put together a circus in his name, taking Andrew Haight as a partner, marking Haight's entry into the circus business.

In his obituary of Haight, W. W. Durand called him the busiest man he ever saw.

> "He was as tireless as time itself. He was the hardest kind of worker, and the most loyal man to his employers.... He was esteemed and popular everywhere, and received large salaries—$5,000 and $6,000 the last few years, most of which he gave away.... He was a great-hearted man, true to his friends and forgiving to his enemies."[41]

Andrew Haight was born near Penn Yan, Yates County, New York, in 1832. His father was a successful

---

41. Durand, "The Late Andrew Haight, Career of a Noted Circus Manager and Agent," New York *Clipper*, February 20, 1886.

merchant, so it was natural that he expressed an interest in business early on. As a young man, he worked in the firm of Stewart & Herkimer in Penn Yan, where he exhibited exceptional qualities as a sales clerk. His next employment was with W. M. & E. H. Purdy, dry goods dealers of Elmira, for a large increase in salary. He was with this house until 1847, when his father, who had two flourishing stores in Dresden, induced him to take charge of one of them. When his father died in 1850, Haight was left to manage both establishments and conducted them successfully for two years.

Then, anticipating better opportunities in the West, he left New York State for Wisconsin. Upon moving to Beaver Dam, he entered into successful businesses, operating two large stores, speculating in real estate and constructing and keeping a hotel there—the Clark House, complete with a poolroom and gambling parlor. He also had a third store and hotel in New London, managed by his brothers.[42]

At the age of thirty-four Haight met George W. DeHaven, who inveigled him into putting up money and entering circus management as a partner. In light of all he had going for him, one wonders why he was interested in such a risky venture. With the war ending, he may have anticipated a box office bonanza from along the rivers, which in most areas had been restricted to only military traffic. And then, of course, the South

---

42. W. W. Durand, Great Eastern route book, 1872. Durand introduced his obituary of Haight with, "For ten years of his life I was Andrew Haight's friend and associate, and for nearly twenty years we had been personally intimate. Therefore it seems fitting that I should undertake the sad duty of telling something of his life."

was now opening up and anxious for traveling entertainments. In any case, because of DeHaven's uncanny ability to get money-men involved, he took the bait.

The 1865 touring season would be a marked change from the previous war years. At the outset, the Confederacy was finished; Sherman's drive through the Carolinas, the surrender at Appomattox and the final capitulation on May 26 marked the end. Now the entire country was open for travel, albeit dangerous in many areas. Shows would quickly expand their routes southward.

At the beginning, at least, Haight and DeHaven had a small outfit—no menagerie, no bandwagon, and no ticket wagon. Band members paraded on horseback and tickets were sold from a raised stand about five feet square. No large number of horses were required since the circus was to be a boat show. DeHaven was the manager and Haight the treasurer. Levi J. North began as the equestrian director; W. McArthur, the ringmaster; and P. H. Seaman, Tom Burgess, and Albert Aymar, clowns. William Naylor did the principal hurdle and somersault work. Signor Bliss performed his ceiling walking act. In addition, there was a "Laughable Ballet Pantomime" performed by what appears to have been the ladies and youngsters in the company. Mlle. Louise ascended the wire outside the canvas, walking the distance of 300 feet to the top of the pavilion, some 50 feet above the ground.[43] Admission was set at 75¢

---

43. Clipping from *Billboard*, no date. Others on the bill were Mlle. DeAuley, equestrienne; Mme. Annette Seaman, wire performer and *danseuse*; Levi J. North, Jr., two-pony rider; Signer Bliss, ceiling-walker; Henry Burdeau and

for adults and 50¢ for children.

The circus, under George W. DeHaven & Co.'s Great United, opened at Beaver Dam on the 10th of April, 1865, just four days prior to the shocking assassination of President Lincoln. Performers must have found it difficult to entertain a nation in mourning. Proprietors surely were discouraged by the distraction's temporary effect at the box office. But "the show must go on" is the everlasting slogan, and indeed it did.

For the remainder of April and into May, DeHaven & Co. played towns in Wisconsin and Minnesota. We are indebted to Dr. Loeffler for research on DeHaven's activity in this part of the country. He states that the company was at St. Paul on May 11, where they received a new canvas pavilion, which could indicate that things were going well. Certainly, they were well received there. "The fact is, a really good company is soon found out, and after the first performance on Thursday afternoon, the news spread over the city that DeHaven had to be the best circus ever brought to St. Paul."[44]

Shortly, DeHaven & Co. moved down the Rock River on the *Jeannette Roberts* and stopped at places along the Mississippi, Missouri, Ohio and adjoining water-

---

Louis Carr, gymnasts; Charles Rivers, general performer; Henry Coyle, stilt-walking clown; and the Bliss family contributing their tumbling skills. J. H. Perkins led the brass band and A. T. Britton had charge of the string band.

44. Robert J. Loeffler, "Visits of George Washington DeHaven and His Circus to St. Paul, Minnesota and Beyond," Part 4, p. 26, *The White Tops*, November/December, 2002, quoting from the St. Paul (MN) *Pioneer and Democrat*, May 12, 1865.

ways. The show suffered a blow-down at McGregor, Iowa, on May 20th. It occurred around 10 P.M. while the minstrel concert was being performed. The storm came up with little warning, causing a great panic within the pavilion. There was thunder, lightning, the breaking of ropes and poles, until finally the tent collapsed on top of the people that had not managed to escape to the outside. The canvas was greatly damaged by the broken poles and by knives of audience members anxious to get out from under.

> "Bonnets, hats, combs, coats, 'waterfalls,' 'rats' (female names for hair appendages), and lots of curiosities were thrown to the winds and lost forever. The struggle to 'get out' was terrific, and oh how it blowed! Report says not less than 100 valuables were lost that night: some went into the river, some were mashed to pieces and some, we regret to say, were *appropriated* by DeHaven's company in picking up the canvas."[45]

The *Jeannette Roberts* steamed up the Missouri and arrived at Leavenworth on June 21, carrying one of the first circuses to enter Kansas following the war. That the show satisfied the entertainment-hungry population can be confirmed by the following passage from the *Daily Conservative* of the 22nd.

---

45. McGregor (IA) *North Iowa Times*, May 24, 1865.

"The seats were filled with some of our best citizens yesterday, and all seemed highly pleased. Those who do not attend the circus will miss a first-class performance. The audience filled the canvass to overflowing last night, and as everybody brings away a good report, all would believe those who desire a seat to go early this afternoon and evening. This is their last day here."[46]

The show was heavily advertised in Kansas. Ads ran seven days in advance of the performance dates in the *Daily Conservative*. This was repeated in Atchison's *Daily Champion* for the appearance in that city. There, J. H. Owens erected a billboard eighty feet long and twelve feet high on the corner of Commerce and Second Streets and filled the space with the showy circus paper. It was announced that, after leaving Atchison, the circus would continue on the Missouri, stopping at St. Joseph for June 26 and 27, and then proceed as far north as Council Bluffs, Iowa, just across the river from Omaha. When the company returned down river, a second stop was made at Leavenworth on July 11, with the *Conservative* expressing gratification on the following day equal to that of the earlier stand.

"The mammoth circus of DeHaven & Co. arrived at our levee on their return on time yesterday morning, and made a triumphant

---

46. Orin C. King, "Only Big Show Coming," Vol. 1, Chapter 1, Part 1, *Bandwagon*, November/December, 1996.

march through our city to their former place of exhibition. Both the performances in the afternoon and evening were well attended. By urgent request, and to accommodate a large number of soldiers, the circus will give three performances at the Fort today—at 9½ a.m., 1½ p.m., and 7½ p.m. We advise all the boys in blue to attend, for it is the best circus ever in this part of the country."[47]

An unexpected and quite astounding episode occurred at the Fort. Following Mlle. Louise's outdoor exhibition on the wire, a drum major of the 14th Illinois Regiment stepped forward and announced he could do better. He was immediately challenged by one of the company, who offered to bet him $25 that he could not walk ten feet up the incline. Boldly accepting the wager, the soldier pulled off his boots and mounted the wire in his stocking feet. The disbelieving showman then made the proposal that if he performed the feat successfully his entire regiment would be passed into the tent at no charge. With this, the soldier walked up the wire to the center pole, made an about face in military fashion, and began his descent. In an act of arrogance, about halfway down he stood on one foot, sticking the other out straight, and then sat down on the wire with both legs extended. After arriving again on solid ground, he was greeted by lusty cheers from his comrades.

That evening the wire-walking drum major arrived

---
47. *Ibid.*

with a number of his regiment expecting to be ushered into the tent for a complimentary performance. To his surprise, the circus people refused to honor their previous offer. With this, quite a row ensued. Four people were knocked to the ground, the treasurer's box was upset, and the canvas was ripped in places. Further damage was forestalled when the soldiers were finally let in.

There were more frightening encounters with local troublemakers, incidents that occurred with greater frequency than in the past. The thousands of soldiers suddenly idled from their warring existence, still armed for battle, but trying to forget the nightmare memories of the last few years, created a volatile climate in isolated communities, suspicious of the encroachment of strangers. John Glenroy recalled that in Missouri nearly everyone carried revolvers and knives, whether on the street or places of business, including waitresses at public dining rooms and barbers in their shops. "It was a common thing to see Negro women walking along the street carrying revolvers in their hands," he wrote.[48] Nevertheless, a Missouri city correspondent, referring to a visit there on June 17, disclosed that the show was "in receipt of lots of greenbacks."

DeHaven & Co. had a long jump on the *Jeannette Roberts* along the Ohio for an August date at Alton, Indiana. Because of arriving at their destination shortly before show time, Mlle. Louise's free act was omitted, as well as Signor Bliss' ceiling walking feat,

---

48. John Glenroy, *Ins and Outs of Circus Life*, p. 141.

with substitutes inserted in their stead. The next stand at Madison, Indiana, was over 150 miles from Alton, so a night performance was not given. Later, when the circus was loading onto their boat, some of the audience came around to express dissatisfaction. Included in this party were a number of soldiers. The demonstration ultimately became a nuisance to the loading process and DeHaven ordered the protesters off the boat. It appeared that the matter was settled; but, when the *Jeannette Roberts* steamed away, the soldiers reappeared and began shooting in her direction. As the boat moved up the Ohio River, the soldiers followed at a distance, sporadically sniping at the pilot house. Although there were seventy or eighty shots fired into the moving craft, there were no serious injuries to the passengers.

Early in August it was announced that the circus was to go from Cairo down river to New Orleans, then to Mobile and up the Alabama River to Montgomery. It would then switch to rail for passage to Augusta and Savannah. At this time the company consisted of Barney and Mrs. Carroll, Sam Lathrop, P. H. Seaman, Tom Burgess, Joseph Tinkham, W. M. Johnson, Charley Rivers, John and William Naylor, L. B. Carr, Henry Burdeau, Signor Bliss, J. H. Pizzarro, George McDonogh, Sam Rhinehart, and his three boys.

At the end of October, Haight sold his hotel at Beaver Dam and bought DeHaven out at Vicksburg, Mississippi, because, it has been said, DeHaven did not consider it judicious to tour in the South. Haight would now go it alone, under the DeHaven title until the advertising paper was used up. The partnership had lasted barely a half-dozen months, but the pair would be together again for another venture in 1871.

With Andrew Haight buying George W. DeHaven & Co. in the fall of 1865, DeHaven now had cash to form another circus for the 1866 season. It was to become DeHaven's Imperial Circus, a title he would manage for the next half-dozen years. If there was a backer or backers for this at the outset, no name has surfaced; but he would need financial help even before the season opened. Poor DeHaven was prone to misfortune in his ventures of management. Before starting on the road in 1866, DeHaven's company was handed a considerable loss of advertising bills and cuts brought about from the burning of the *Enquirer* office in Cincinnati, along with other structures, a collateral casualty of the great Opera House fire.

The fire broke out in Pike's Opera House, which was considered one of the most splendid venues of entertainment in the West. Although the building was completely destroyed, it was most fortunate that the night's program—"Midsummer Night's Dream"—was over and the audience dispersed. It was thought that the conflagration was started at about 11:30 P.M. by a gas explosion near the backstage scenery. The Cincinnati *Commercial* reported:

> "In five minutes the flames had wrapped the whole magnificent interior of stage and auditorium, and burst through the rear portion

of the roof. On the wings of the draught thus provided, the flames shot up to a great height and lapped over upon adjoining buildings. Soon huge masses of black smoke burst from the cornice of the Fourth Street front windows. At a quarter of twelve the scene was exciting in the extreme. The half square bounded by Fourth, Vine, Baker, and Walnut streets had a dome of luridly gleaming flames, through which columns of smoke shot up, and from which showers of sparks and bunches of flames floated upward and then descended upon the burning mass below. The dome and ceiling, with their gorgeous and artistic ornamentation, fell with the roof with a terrific crash, and there burst upward a dazzling light, blinding in its intensity. Slowly but surely the fire crept down through the various stories of the edifice—through offices and studios—steadily down to the magnificent stores, running the entire length of the building on the first floor of Fourth Street into the wealth of literature, the tens of thousands worth of books of CARROLL's store, the valuable stock of SUNNER'S sewing machines, the fine music-store of W. C. PETERS, and Philip Philip's pianos, the immense goods stored in the Adams Express rooms, the college rooms of BRYANT, STRATTON, & DE HAN's Commercial Institute, the editorial room of the National Union.

HARPEL'S job printing establishment, with its valuable machinery, and all the dozen offices besides. From the real and west side of the Opera-house the flames marched with overwhelming strength to the extensive stables of the Adams Express Company and the buildings of the Cincinnati *Daily Enquirer*. The fall of a large mass of wall upon the rear of the *Enquirer* building insured its partial destruction, and soon the flames were communicated to the rear of the first and second floors, and rushing onward crept through the front windows, and told the story of their power to the fireman, who crept up to grapple with them. But with the same power already so terribly used the devouring flames wrapped the structure in their embrace, and the work of destruction was soon far advanced through the job rooms, where were stored nearly $100,000 worth of cuts; through job-presses, and composing-rooms of JONES & HART—all totally destroyed."[49]

The loss was estimated at $1,751,000, over half of which was Pike's Opera House. However, for DeHaven's circus, scheduled to open on May 5, it was a setback of about $8,000. As if this was not enough, the specially made pavilion, a $3,000 value, was ignited by a spark from the engine and burned on its railway car while en route to St. Paul. Although it was fully

---
49. *Harper's Weekly*, April 14, 1866, quoting the *Cincinnati Enquirer*.

insured, the accident delayed the opening. An item in the *Pioneer and Democrat* of May 6 read, "Notwithstanding the reverses sustained by the Company, they are all still undaunted, and busily making arrangements for their summer tour."[50]

The 1866 season was eventually launched at Minneapolis on May 21 with new canvas, new seats and other new paraphernalia, and with a strong troupe of performers. There were the internationally recognized equestrienne Madame Louise Tourniaire and her brother, hurdle rider Theodore; Mlle. Kate Bailey, wire-walker and ascensionist; gymnasts Louis B. Carr and Henry Burdeau; rider William Dutton; leaper George Batcheller; acrobat Burnell Runnells and his two boys; somersaulter Sam Rhinehart; and two experienced clowns in William Worrell and P. S. Seaman. Fred Bailey was the agent.

The artistic level of the company was immediately confirmed by the St. Paul *Pioneer and Democrat* of May 23. "We believe it is the opinion of all who were present that the performance of this Company cannot be equaled. Madame Tourniaire, Master William Dutton, and Monsieur Burnell fully sustained their high reputation, while the two boys, sons of Monsieur Burnell, excited the wonder and admiration of all."[51]

Following the St. Paul opening, DeHaven & Co., a river show, played dates in Minnesota and Wisconsin; then in June, moved down the Mississippi, stopping

---

50. St. Paul (MN) *Pioneer and Democrat*, May 6, 1866.

51. Loeffler, Part 5, p. 26, *The White Tops*, January/February, 2003, quoting from the St. Paul (MN) *Pioneer and Democrat*, May 24, 1866.

at the major junctions along the way—Dubuque, Davenport, Rock Island, Burlington, Hannibal, etc. We learn in a report from the latter city that the June 14 performance there was highly rewarding. "Occasionally Hannibal, like larger cities, is favored with a first-class circus. Geo. W. DeHaven & Co.'s Imperial Circus exhibited here last night, and we can say without fear of contradiction, that it was the circus of the season." The writer found Mme. Tourniaire to be a woman "of noble beauty and pleasing address" and the most accomplished equestrienne presently before the public. William Worrell was considered "the only witty, chaste and original jester" who has appeared in Hannibal in many years. Also commended was the riding of William Dutton, George Batcheller and Henry North, but the highest praise was saved for a trio of gymnasts, Burnell Runnels and his two little boys in classic groupings and posturings.

In late June, DeHaven & Co. moved up the Missouri to St. Joseph, Leavenworth and Kansas City, also drawing approval from the local scribes. "DeHaven says he has the best organization which has ever exhibited in the West," wrote a man from the Leavenworth *Daily Conservative*, "and after witnessing the performances yesterday we believe him." Mme. Tourniaire's skills on an unbridled barebacked horse "were absolutely thrilling," and her ménage act excelled anything seen before.[52]

But on July 1 an item appeared in the *Conservative*

---

52. Leavenworth (KS) *Daily Conservative*, June 30, 1866.

that for barely a year after the war is to this writer utterly astounding and admirably bold; and we feel compelled to enter it here in its entirety.

"Now that DeHaven's circus has closed its performances here, we have an opportunity to make some suggestions relative to the conduct of circuses in general, without rendering ourselves liable to the imputation of a design to injure the business of this particular one.

"Since the days when the glaring and highly colored bills of these shows filled our youthful breast with admiration, and awakened therein a painful longing, which could only be satisfied with the realization of the promised pleasure—we say, since those days we never recollect of having never attended a circus in which the negro, or 'nigger,' as the disciples of the saw-dust circle classically name him, was not made the target of the coarsest allusions, and the victim of barbarous jokes which had not wit enough to redeem them from absolute blackguardism.

"It is time these low-lived and beastly practices be stopped. When colored men, and women, and children visit a circus, they pay their money like white folks, and we have always observed that they behave themselves equally as well. The badge of inferiority is made sufficiently apparent by huddling them together in a particular portion of the amphitheatre, without subjecting them to the brutality of those fellows in striped garments, who, being employed to play the fool, generally seem to be qualified by nature for the *role*. The sort of humor which delights in ridiculing a poor and defenseless people never excites the risibilities of the true lady or gentleman, and is scarcely ever met save with the loud guffaw of the shameless courtesan, and the masculine blackguards who are equally shameless.

"When one of DeHaven's clown perpetrated the stale pun, 'You can rob a white man of his last penny, but you can't rob a nigger of his last *scent*,' the decent portion of the audience seemed to shudder, while the portion that was not so decent were in ecstasies. And when the same clown, seeing a respectably dressed and modest appearing colored woman walking around the side of the amphitheatre towards the place assigned to her, pursued her with his mock and insulting manner, he should have been forthwith hissed from the ring.

"This is not the day, nor is Kansas the place for such exhibitions of contempt for the negro. They belong to the age of woman-whipping and baby-selling, and seem to be perennial in a Kentucky or South Carolina climate. The people here are inclined to let the negro alone, to protect him from oppression, to encourage him to honest industry, and to afford him every facility for improving and elevating his condition by his own exertions. Being so disposed, no one approves this abuse and ridicule of the negro, except such as have reason to be jealous of his superiority.

"As a whole, Mr. DeHaven's circus is one of the best that travels, and we only throw out these hints that it may be still further improved by the elimination of these obnoxious features, and that those which are to follow may avoid their use."[53]

July was an unfortunate time for DeHaven & Co. An accident befell the show in Kansas City where several people were injured when on July 2 a section of the seats collapsed. At Waverly, Missouri, on the 9th the troupers were attacked by a party of ruffians and robbed of their money and watches. "The attack was unprovoked on the part of the circus company, being made while they were passing through the town on the way to their boat." Four of the group were captured.[54]

At St. Louis, the stand was advertised for three days beginning July 16, with the proceeds of a July 18 performance to be donated to the relief of Southern sufferers. But the actors, having not seen salaries for some time, balked at participating in such a charity. The *Missouri Republican* reported the disagreement the following day.

---

53. Leavenworth (KS) *Daily Conservative*, July 1, 1866.
54. Loeffler, Part 5, p. 28, quoting the *Missouri Republican*.

"Yesterday afternoon a large crowd gathered under the spacious canvas of DeHaven's circus to witness the performance, which, however, owing to an unforeseen imbroglio between the actors and the proprietors, did not take place. It appears that a strike took place among the former and they refused to go on through their evolutions. The origin of the difficulty is said to be arrears of salary due to the actors. The proceeds of the performances were said to be given to the Southern Relief Association. The employees proposed to the proprietors that if they would rescind this decision and distribute the amount among them they would go through with the performance and do their best to please the assemblage. The proposition was refused, and negotiations were broken off between the belligerent parties, and the authorities were informed that the exhibition could not go forward, and that the admission money would be returned at the entrance, which was done without serious trouble, except sundry expressions of disapprobation on the part of small boys."[55]

With the assistance of the sheriff, who impounded some of the horses, the company prevailed on management to make a settlement in their favor.

Instead of three days, the show remained a week and then suspended to re-organize. Henry Burdeau and

---

55. *Ibid.*

H. C. North left to connect with Haight & Chambers. William Dutton and John Murphy joined Lake's Hippo-Olympiad. The featured performers now consisted of Mme. Tourniaire and daughter, Burnell Runnells and two sons, and Le June Burt. On leaving the city, Messrs. Louder and Webb were the managers and a Mr. Cropsey was said to have put up some money. Shortly, Webb withdrew.

After a stand in Cairo, DeHaven & Co. went up the Ohio River, working towns on both the Ohio and Kentucky sides of the river—Paducah, Henderson, Evansville, Louisville, etc. Then, in early September, our boat travelers turned south on the Tennessee and, following a series of estuaries, ended up at Nashville for a four-day stop. According to the *Clipper*, the show returned to the Ohio and made a final run up as far as Cincinnati. This presumably ended the season. In October it was reported that: "Taken altogether the season has been a prosperous one, and but two companies have met with bad business. These are the Thayer & Noyes party and George DeHaven's show."[56] Poor DeHaven had done it again.

After closing, DeHaven arranged the construction of what was described as a "commodious and comfortable" amphitheatre in St. Paul on Sixth Street between Minnesota and Wabash, where a series of entertainments was initiated during the Christmas holidays. DeHaven was the manager; C. R. Haines, the treasurer; William Dutton, equestrian manager; H. F. Nichols,

---

56. New York *Clipper*, October 20, 1866.

master of the circle; and P. H. Seaman, the clown.

The circus building was erected with local money; and, according to the home town paper, DeHaven took unto himself a local bride.

> "Mr. George DeHaven having married one of our St. Paul girls is now a St. Paul man. Vetale Guerin, David Guerin, John B. Oliver and others are all St. Paul residents and having few amusements here during the winter months deserve well for setting up at such expense a comfortable and respectable place of amusement. Those who are fond of the sports and arts of the ring will find a visit to DeHaven's a pleasant way of spending an evening."[57]

The regular season began on Tuesday, January 1, 1867, with performances occurring every Wednesday and Saturday. A week later an item in the *Pioneer and Democrat* informed the residents of St. Paul:

> "The Imperial Circus under the auspices of DeHaven & Co., consisting of some of the most enterprising citizens has been opened with signal success, and its managers feel gratified with the results. During the holidays they had crowded houses, and both nights of last week were more than satisfactory. Messrs. DeHaven & Co. have spared no pains and expense to make the hippodrome attractive, and we do not

---

57. St. Paul (MN) *Pioneer and Democrat*, January 9, 1867.

hesitate to commend it as a proper place for parents and children to spend an afternoon or evening."

On January 16 the paper abruptly announced that the company had deferred its weekly performances until the arrival of their entire equestrian troupe, which was to be within a few days. What is happening here? The re-opening did not occur until January 26. But to everyone's misfortune, on about 10:30 that evening a fire broke out in the Mansion House on the corner of Wabash and Fifth Streets. The building was completely destroyed within a few hours. Two fire engines responded to the call, but, once at the site, had difficulty in getting a sufficient amount of hose, losing some twenty minutes before water could be applied. The building was nothing but a pile of ashes by 1:00 A.M. The circus performers who were staying there suffered losses, the greatest being to P. H. Seaman and the Milson Brothers, whose several hundred dollars worth of wardrobe was committed to the pyre; although a benefit given for them a week later helped to allay the calamity.

An item of the 27th indicated that new actors had arrived. And another on February 1 issued high praise for the company and announced that "the clown who was burnt out at the Mansion house and lost all he had is to have a benefit on Saturday night, when we trust he will have a good house."

The six-week winter season ended on March 24 unprofitably. According to the *Clipper*, "Financial misunderstanding in a number of places had a bad influence when ventilated by newspapers, which led the people to think that his show 'did not amount to much'," which partially explains the circus' dilemma. But quite the contrary, the item went on to explained, "he gives a good performance, and has talent that will compare favorably with any in the saw-dust arena."[58]

DeHaven's Imperial Circus went on the road under the proprietorship of David Guerin and Charles R. Haines for the 1867 summer season, this time by rail (by July 19 Haines was no longer a partner). DeHaven was manager; J. B. Oliver, treasurer; Oliver Bell, equestrian director; and H. F. Nichols, master of the ring; C. McCumber, director of advertising; J. O. Davis, general agent; and the performing roster included several of the people who had been a part of the winter season. Admissions were 50¢ and 25¢.

The show was at St. Paul on May 18; dates followed in Minnesota and Wisconsin. We can get an idea of the circus program from a May advertisement for Oscoola Mills, Wisconsin. The ad revealed the following entertainments. Annie Worland made the outdoor ascension to the music of Capt. J. Ollerenshaw's Metropolitan Opera Band. Within the pavilion she rode the principal act, leaping through banners and other standard feats of that genre, and later showed her ability on the slack-wire. DeHaven, billed as "The most Thorough, Practical, Efficient and Humane Horse Tamer on the Continent," exhibited the trained horse, Pilot. Mme.

---

58. New York *Clipper*, June 8, 1867.

Worland was featured for her daring and accomplished feats of equestrianism. William Dutton, her counterpart, performed on his flying barebacked steed and, in addition, made a leap for life from a springboard. Oliver Bell did his specialty of throwing a somersault through a hoop lined with pointed daggers. The Milson Brothers presented a variety of gymnastics, acrobatics and muscular achievements. P. H. Seaman was back heading the clown department, assisted by W. A. McArthur. The Lafontaine Brothers, Henry and Alfred, added their gymnastic and acrobatic elements as well. Finally, there was Master Henry, a "juvenile prodigy," working the horizontal bars.[59]

Who was this Master Henry? He could have been one of the aforementioned Lafontaines or possibly the seven-year-old son of Vital Guerin. Loeffler has noted that young Henry Guerin performed the free act of walking a rope to the top of the tent at St. Paul. With his brother, David, as part of the DeHaven cavalcade, it is logical for the boy, if talented in that direction, to be with it.

The show crossed Michigan on its way to Canada and Maine. A July date in Detroit was well attended and well received. After Maine the company backtracked across Canada, where there was a switch to wagon travel before alighting again on U.S. soil at Ogdensburgh, New York, on September 17. More dates

---

59. An advertisement, Portland (ME), August 21, 1867, lists the following performers: Luke Rivers, William Dutton, Oliver Bell, Lafontaine Brothers, P. H. Seaman, Annie Worland, Thomas O'Brian, E. Schofield, G. W. DeHaven, Madame Worland, Gus Lee, Master Henry, and La Petite Annie.

in New York State followed.

The season was marred by the death of Oliver Bell. He was drowned, supposedly by walking off the boat in the darkness of the night while the company was crossing Three Rivers in Canada. Sadly, his body was not found until five days later, washed some three miles below the place of crossing. It was buried in a small community near the spot of discovery.

William Shephard was the money man DeHaven unearthed for the 1868 season. Under his proprietorship, DeHaven was manager; R. D. Moody, treasurer; Oliver Dodge, ringmaster; Frank Equirrel, band leader; and C. McCumber, general agent. Admissions were 40¢ and 25¢. Featured in advertisements were Charles Bliss, the human fly, and his sons Albert, Charles and George; the Worland family, Mme. Jerry Worland, Annie and little Johnny, back for a second season; Madame Bridges, the celebrated bareback and pad rider from Paris; E. Scofield & Gillum, acrobats; Joseph Tinkham, hurdle rider; Luke Rivers, scenic rider; DeHaven's trick horse, Pilot; and a school of trained horses. J. C. Wallace and Gus Lee were the clowns, "who vie with one another in witty sayings, and it is difficult to decide which of them bears away the palm." The outside attraction was performed by Annie and Johnny Worland.

DeHaven & Co. started out at Macomb, Illinois on May 1 and followed with dates in Iowa, Minnesota, and Wisconsin. W. Quinette Hendricks was with the company, giving us the only personal recollection of the season. We repeat it here with the warning to the reader that his recollections are sometimes suspect. He stated that he joined at Cincinnati on April 24 as clown and talker for the sideshow. Travel was by steamboat on the Ohio and Mississippi, the *Will S. Hayes*, a stern-wheeler equipped with a calliope. The incomplete routing information available confirms there were dates along the Mississippi in May.

Hendricks stated the show arrived at Milwaukee by rail on July 4:

> "We remained there for one whole week while the company was getting a steamer ready for us to make a tour of the lakes. When the steamer arrived from Chicago, the *John J. Rowe*, they put all the show aboard her, horses and all. She was a large boat, driven by propeller. So we took that boat and went on a tour of the lakes, making all the towns on Lake Michigan, Lake Superior, Lake Erie, and arriving at Buffalo, New York, we took railroads again and toured the eastern states."[60]

This included various towns in Canada.

At Buffalo, where the tent was pitched on the corner of Niagara and Pearl Streets, the August 5 *Courier* rated the performances "of the finest order of merit." The writer was impressed with Annie Worland, who, speeding around the ring "was the most graceful little creature imaginable." She appeared on the tight-

---
60. W. Quinette Hendricks, *Stranger Than Fiction*.

rope "with a recklessness and abandon never seen equaled, and which is especially remarkable considering her tender years." Charles Bliss' ceiling walking also caught his attention. "Many think this part of the performance is a humbug, merely put upon the bills to draw a crowd, but we can assure all doubters that Mr. Bliss really performs the feat. How he does it is a mystery." The Cleveland *Plain Dealer* reported on August 8 that the show had appeared the previous day to a "fair audience" and had given "universal satisfaction."

September found the show in Michigan. After arriving in Flint by railroad on September 8, rainy weather eliminated an afternoon performance. A further unfortunate situation was caused by competition with Yankee Robinson's circus, which was billed to be in Flint on the 22nd. The rivalry continued on with the route through Fenton, Clinton, Ann Arbor, Howell, etc.

A *Clipper* item in July stated the season for tented shows suffered from unfavorable weather. From the outset there was a disagreeable cold spell accompanied by constant rain. Many of the roadways were either cut up or washed away, forcing delay in movement and, in some cases, canceled dates. "George DeHaven commenced at Macomb, Ill.," it read, "but has not made any money."[61] We suspect that continued throughout the tour before going into winter quarters at Lincoln, Illinois.

---

61. New York *Clipper*, July 18, 1868.

Alderman and Ladd were the proprietors for DeHaven & Co.'s Combination Circus for 1869. As usual, DeHaven was manager. In addition, there were William Alderman, treasurer; Barney Carroll, equestrian director; Prof. Fisher, band director; Sam Joseph, general agent. Mme. Eloise Bridges returned as the principal equestrienne. In addition, there were the Lazelle Brothers, the Carroll family, Joseph Tinkham, Oliver Dodge, clowns Sam Lathrop and William Anderson, etc. Charles Meyers, with his educated hog, had the sideshow.

The season began at the Academy of Music in Bloomington, Illinois, for a week on the 19th of April. On the 26th the circus opened under canvas at nearby Lincoln. "DeHaven's Imperial Circus which has been quartering in this city during the past winter, gave the first exhibition under canvas on Monday last. They gave a very creditable performance."[62]

Although the routing information available for 1869 is sketchy, we can presume that from Lincoln, which was located along Salt Creek, the company navigated the Sangamon and Illinois rivers, then up the Ohio and Mississippi, making use of the *Will S. Hayes*, a sternwheeler equipped with a calliope, as they played towns in Illinois and Iowa during April and May.

Minnesota and Wisconsin were visited in June and July. At an appearance in St. Paul on June 10 the sheriff intervened and held the outfit for a debt that DeHaven had run up three years prior, this due to an

---

62. New York *Clipper*, April 24, 1869.

unpaid bill for costumes and the unfortunate burning of the canvas and advertising paper.

The Minneapolis *Tribune* recorded the event: "After the performance last night Deputy Sheriff Grace attached the canvas of DeHaven's Circus to satisfy a claim of $400 held by Charles Lacker: a tailor on Jackson Street, who made costumes for DeHaven in 1866.... The claim might, perhaps, be settled, were it not that other attachments to the amount of several thousand dollars await the result of this, to be laid upon the same property." DeHaven protested, claiming he did not own the show, but merely received a salary for his services. The matter was said to have been "privately" settled.[63]

Travel in Minnesota and Wisconsin took up most of June and July. Indiana and Ohio were visited in August and September. A *Clipper* reporter stated that the company had enjoyed good business since entering Indiana, and added, "They have one of the best railroad shows I have ever seen."[64] The quality was enhanced at this time by the addition of the Runnells family and popular clown Jimmy Reynolds.

The Cincinnati *Daily Enquirer* reported a three-day stand in that city, September 16-18, to have pleased and delighted audiences. "Among the *attaches* of this organization will be found the most famous artists that have ever visited this city." The act of child rider, little Annie Carroll, and the feats of Burnell Runnells

---

63. Loeffler, Part 7, p. 29, *The White Tops*, May/June, 2003, quoting from the St. Paul (MN) *Pioneer and Democrat*, June 12, 1869.

64. New York *Clipper*, September 4, 1869.

and sons drew special mention. On the third day of the engagement the proceeds of the two performances were to be the rewards of a benefit tendered to the general agent, Sam Joseph.[65]

The tour ended at Springfield, Ohio, on November 15. In reference to DeHaven & Co., a *Clipper* summary of the circus season in late October read, "The receipts of this show have been too small to allow a profit to anyone."[66] Sadly, it was a typical ending for poor DeHaven.

Now at last, our story's third protagonist comes into view, as DeHaven went out for the season of 1870 in partnership with R. E. J. Miles of Cincinnati, well known in theatrical circles.

Miles had toured in the United States and Canada, amassing a considerable fortune. "Colonel Miles in *Mazeppa* was for years one of the best known character actors on the stage," M. B. Leavitt wrote in his *Fifty Years in Theatrical Management*. "His Dick Turtin was regarded as a marvelous bit of acting in those days and he brought a score of other characters, compelling the admiration of the public by the artistic excellence of his impressions."

In 1867 Miles took possession of Cincinnati's National Theatre, where he offered to the public such stars as Edwin Booth, Joseph Jefferson and Edwin Forrest. So in 1870, as DeHaven's partner, he brought with him solid experience in matters of theatrical

---

65. Cincinnati (OH) *Daily Enquirer*, September 18, 1869.

66. New York *Clipper*, October 10, 1869.

presentation and management.

Early advertisements of the DeHaven-Miles organization listed a strong company of equestrians, athletes and gymnasts. Included were the aerobatic feats of the Davenport Brothers; Mlle. Zuleila, female gymnast and "aerial fairy"; Kate and Ella, the beautiful equestrienne daughters of Spencer Q. Stokes; Mlle. Le Burte. "dramatic and equestrienne artist"; S. Q. Stokes and his trained ponies; riders James Wilson, Charles Lowery and Mons. Vantini; Signor Bliss and family; Mons. Ricardo, a "Modern Samson"; and clowns Jimmy Reynolds, P. H. Seaman and Mons. Vantini. The educated horse, Comet, made his return, supported by two mules, Humpty Dumpty and Shoo Fly. A special feature was a production of *Mazeppa*, with Mlle. Le Burte in the title role.

Mazeppa was a popular equestrian drama, adapted from Lord Byron's lengthy poem, published in June of 1819. Byron had based his *Mazeppa* on Voltaire's *The History of Charles XII, King of Sweden*, which, in turn, was taken from a real life incident. The drama was especially popular when the hero was portrayed by an actress, who sensationalized it in wearing fleshlings that simulated nakedness and displayed every contour of the body. Charlotte Crampton (Mrs. Wilkinson) was the first of a line of female Mazeppas, described as a petite young woman, with an exquisite form and handsome face. She made her debut in the role on January 3, 1859, at New York's Chatham Theatre, where she introduced her trained horses, Alexander and Black

Eagle. Perhaps in an attempt to outdo her male counterparts she went up the "run" without being lashed to the horse, a feat that had not been done before in the piece.

The most noted of these male imitators was Adah Isaacs Menken. It wasn't until 1861, however, that she became an overnight star by performing in *Mazeppa, the Wild Horse of Tartary* at the Green Street Theatre in Albany. This was followed by tours in the United States and Europe, earning for her the highest salary paid to an actress at that time. Other female Mazeppas followed—Kate Fisher, Helene Smith, Kate Vance, Fanny Louise Buckingham, Kate Raymond, Madame Sanyeah, etc.

DeHaven's *Mazeppa* was obviously advertised to take advantage of this contemporary craze. It was probably proposed by Miles, who quite suitably arranged and staged it, drawing on his experience as a horse drama performer and former touring star in the piece. But for now, it was Mlle. Le Burte who carried the show, which was presented, an ad read, "with their magnificent wardrobe in all its splendor and grandeur." This may have included the costumes that Miles had used for his touring production some years earlier.

The circus featured a balloon ascension as an outdoor free act, replacing the traditional wire-walking. The balloon had became a popular attraction in the years following the Civil War, and DeHaven & Co. were the first circus to use it. W. W. Durand, in his brief biography of Miles in the 1872 Great Eastern Route Book, makes the forceful claim that R. E. J. Miles was "the undisputed father of the sensation, and to him alone is the credit due."[67] The practice began this season with no fanfare and seemingly no thought of it being innovative. The first indication of its use was carried in the *Clipper* of that year. "One of the aeronauts connected with DeHaven's Circus was recently severely injured by falling from the balloon into a summer house at Davenport, Iowa, and his substitute was drowned at Dubuque by falling in the river, we are informed."

The company moved along the major rivers that bordered Iowa, Illinois and Indiana on the boat *Victor #4*.[68] At Quincy on June 3 the event brought a large crowd to the grounds for the afternoon show. According to the *Daily Herald's* report of June 4: "At the appointed time the balloon, inflated with heated air, rose majestically upward for a few hundred yards, and floated off in an eastern direction, and came down with a rush in the vicinity of the hospital. Prof. Strong, who was in the basket, was jammed up considerably from the force with which he came to the ground, but was all right last evening."

The writer called the arenic performance "meritorious and far above the average." Of particular mention were clown Jimmy Reynolds, Zuleila, the female gymnast and "aerial fairy," and the Davenport brothers. He then added, "The management and the

---

67. Durand, 1872 Great Eastern Route Book.

68. The *Victor #4*, under the command of Capt. Uriah B. Scott, was christened in 1866. Its size was 171 x 25.5 x 4.5, 286 tons. Frederick Way, *Way's Packet Directory*, item 5566.

company are courteous, honorable and gentlemanly, and we recommend them to the kind consideration of the press and public wherever they may go."[69]

At the end of July, R. E. J. Miles, who had been a co-proprietor, purchased the circus, which continued to function under the DeHaven banner. We can only assume that DeHaven remained as manager. The company traveled the Ohio River until it reached Wheeling, West Virginia, when it was transferred to moving on the Baltimore and Ohio Railroad.

At Wheeling it was reported that the balloon ascension drew a huge crowd. "It is wonderful how many people will turn out to see a show," the *Daily Intelligence* observed, "when it costs nothing." Also noted was that the lady advertised to go up in it "wore a splendid pair of whiskers." Nevertheless, some 2,000 people were on hand to witness the evening performance, which was judged *very fair*. "We do not hanker, however, after a repetition of the thrilling spectacle of the *Mazeppa*. It's too exciting. Soda water is not more so."

The paper announced that the show was to leave the *Victor* and go by rail before returning to river travel again at some point. September and October were devoted to the southeastern part of the country before entering into competition with other circuses in the Deep South. But the *Clipper* indicated in November there were too many of them touring in that territory, no less than nine. There was little demand for cotton

---

69. Quincy (IL) *Daily Herald*, June 4, 1870.

at this time and the war in Europe had put a damper on faith in the economy. James M. Nixon's Circus was in Alabama and Mississippi; C. T. Ames' in Georgia; G. G. Grady's in Alabama; Noyes & Van Amburgh's in Tennessee; Stowe's in Mississippi; Cooper, Hemming & Whitby's in Mississippi; Stone & Murray's in Mississippi; and J. W. Robinson's in Mississippi. Miles, with the former DeHaven outfit, also moved into Mississippi and supposedly went broke at Brandon in November.

At the first of the year R. E. J. Miles joined Agnes Lake's Hippo-Olympiad as general director for a two-month winter season in the South. The circus carried a strong company which included Agnes and Emma Lake, Minnie and Hiram Marks, Charles Lowery, Charles Melville, the Lascelles Brothers, clown John Davenport, etc. Horace Nichols was equestrian director; Levi J. North was master of the circle; J. S. Totten, treasurer. Miles also made quick use of his propensity for a balloon ascension as a free act, for it was announced that at 1 P.M. each day, shortly before the start of the matinee, Prof. J. W. Hayden fired up his equipment and went aloft.

The spectacle of *Mazeppa, Wild Horse of Tartary* was featured, in which, the ad read, "MME. AGNES will appear in her original role of Mazeppa, supported by the well known Equestrian Actor, R. E. J. MILES, and a full and efficient Dramatic Company." Agnes was, to use a theatrical expression, "up in the piece," having performed it many times from an adaptation for the ring arranged by her husband. In 1865 she went to Germany for a special appearance in Berlin, thus establishing her as a Mazeppa of international reputation.

A January *Clipper* indicated the company had been doing very fair business in New Orleans. This must have been prior to an engagement at Mobile beginning on January 2 for three days. The show then followed a route into Georgia, Florida, South Carolina, then back into Georgia before disbanding for the winter in Atlanta on February 25. After which, the Hippo-Olympiad returned to Cincinnati.

R. E. J. Miles remained as director of Lake's Hippo-Olympiad for the summer season. This final tour under that title covered a vast area. Beginning in Ohio, the show followed with Illinois and Iowa, then by rail to Nebraska, Colorado, Utah, Idaho, back to Kansas, into Missouri, Illinois, Indiana, closing at Cincinnati, and into winter quarters across the river in Newport, Kentucky.

Circuses that rushed to the South after the Civil War proved there was money to spend for good entertainment. They performed throughout the winter of 1865 for the first time since the start of armed conflict; and, as has nearly always been the case following a war, people made considerable sacrifices for entertainment to distract them from the hardships incident thereto. The major shows touring in that territory at this time were Haight's United States Circus, Thayer & Noyes United States Circus, Seth B. Howes' European Circus, and Dan Castello's Great Show.

Shortly after buying out DeHaven in the fall of 1865 Andrew Haight moved the show to Louisiana. He was in Algiers October 27 and 28, before going across the river to Tivoli Circle, New Orleans, on October 30, where he played to good business through November 4. A move was made to another part of the city, Congo Square, for performances on the 6th through the 10th. "The canvas at Congo Square was crowded last night with an admiring audience, assembled to witness the entertaining and wonderful performances given by the talented troupe of the DeHaven & Co.'s Circus."[70]

The show then moved to Mobile for a six-day stand beginning November 13. The Thayer & Noyes circus came to town for a five-day stand on the following day. A letter to *Clipper* proprietor Frank Queen from Haight, dated Shreveport, February 17, 1866, is indicative of the competition that occurred between the two shows.

> "Hearing of the statement made by Thayer & Noyes party in one of your late issues, and not being able to find the paper, I write you for reference. I understand that Messrs. Thayer & Noyes claim to have taken fifteen thousand dollars ($15,000) during their stay at Mobile, my company being there at the same time, and say that I took but four thousand dollars ($4,000). Both companies played there one

---

70. Loeffler, Part 4, p. 28, quoting from the New Orleans (LA) *Southern Star*, November 8, 1865.

week, opposite each other. Now I contradict this, for I am thoroughly acquainted with the receipts of each company. The above gentlemen and myself paid the internal revenue tax at the same time, and their receipts were $15,000 from the time they left Chattanooga, Tenn., until the last day of their stay at Mobile, which was about three weeks or more. My receipts were $4,000 at Mobile alone. I do not think they took any more money than I did in the five days in the last place. This statement I claim to be true, or else they made a false one to the tax collector."

The letter was signed "A. Haight, Proprietor of G. W. DeHaven & Co.'s Circus."[71]

Haight's organization achieved the distinction of becoming the first to take a circus into Texas after the war. Following the date in Mobile, the former DeHaven's United States Circus shipped out of New Orleans on the *Magnolia* for Galveston, arriving in time to set up their tents for the evening performance

---

71. New York *Clipper*, March 2, 1912. Haight's reaction was the result of an item in the Mobile *Daily Times* of December 15. "Amusement statistics—the books of the assessor and collector of the two percent tax for the United States revenue, on the gross receipts of exhibitions, enabling us to give the proceeds of the three circuses that exhibited here last month.... Thayer & Noyes paid two percent upon the receipts of $15,453 for five days, commencing Nov. 14. DeHaven paid two percent upon the receipts of $4,903.70, for six days, commencing Nov. 13. S. B. Howes paid two percent upon $8,813.55, for two weeks commencing Nov. 20." New York *Clipper*, February 17, 1912. There had been an ongoing feud between the organizations of S. B. Howes and Thayer & Noyes.

on Saturday, November 24. After sending their band out, the patrons, at $1.00 each, crowded into the tent, a rush that amounted to a return of $1,600, plus an additional $400 from the minstrel sideshow. From billing the town on Sunday, the Monday take totaled $2,200 and $575; Tuesday, $2,350 and $600.

The company then went by rail to Houston for December 1, 2, 4, 5—Friday Saturday, Monday, Tuesday. On the 2nd the Houston edition of the Galveston *Daily News* carried this welcoming item.

> "The Circus has Come! Hurrah! All the world, especially the juvenile portion, was in motion yesterday and last night to witness the magnificent performances of the Great United Circus Company. The unrivaled feats of Mlle. Marie, Signor Bliss, etc., commanded universal applause. 'Old Sam Lathrop' and his assistants gave their hearers many hearty laughs. Of course 'Willie the Pet' met with the approval of all. But go and see by all means and remove the wrinkles from your face."

The paper was also commendatory in its view of the circus personnel. "The Company is gentlemanly throughout. A due regard is paid by them to refinement of taste. A Circus Company nearly always at once attracts or repulses the feelings of a community. This one has done the former perfectly; and their visit to the city will be remembered with pleasure."[72]

---

72. Galveston *Daily News*, December 2 and 3, 1865. "Willie the pet"

A letter to the *Clipper* from a member of the company, dated Red River, February 15, is an enlightening portrait of their situation.

"I now sit down to give you a little insight of our travels in Texas. We arrived in Galveston on the 25th of November, and played there five days to overflowing houses; thence to Houston where we turned away people; took railroad to Richmond, and there hired transportation on through to San Antonio, where we played one week to crowded houses, including Sunday. We then bought some horses and hired the rest, and set out through the wilds of Texas on towards Shreveport, La., and of all countries this beats all. Talk of Hottentots, cannibals, barbarians! Here they are everything but civilized, whooping and hollowing, shooting, and all come to the show with pistols and knives; they shoot through the canvas, and call you names that are not very pleasant to hear, and we have to take it all. We had no fuss with them, as we dare not open our mouths. They shoot all around us as we go to and from the canvas. Once in a while we come across a man that knows something, but not often.

"We have now our own conveyances. Our admission here was $1 in specie, or $1.50 in greenbacks, though we don't see many

---

referred to the petite Master William, whom Barney Caroll used in his carrying act.

greenbacks, only where the Union soldiers are. For the horses, all we could get was corn, and poor at that. The horses all stand out doors. You can always find a shingle up at a grocery, go in and you will find a barrel of fighting whiskey made here, and it will kill two hundred yards at sight, also a few cards of gingerbread and some oysters.

"But after all we have made money, and eats, are paid every Sunday. Old man Haight pays up good; he is going to make a good showman; this is his first season. He started from Beaver Dam, Wisconsin, last April, and has run ever since….

"We had three horses stolen from us in Bellevue, first town out of Henderson. We opened in Shreveport, La., on Feb. 12th, after a long and tedious journey among the Yah-hoos and Gillipens, who would put a six-shooter in your mouth and ask you if that was good for a ticket, and one half the time in mud and the other half quarreling to get something to eat. We came out safe and sound and brought all our stock with us, but it was quite a difficulty on our part to do so.

"The company are all well, and start for Mobile Feb. 18th. Mrs. Maginley (Mary Carroll) is riding a splendid act better than ever, and has made a tremendous hit in Shreveport. Barney Carroll is with the company, and is looking as young as ever, leaping over eight and nine horses every day. Ben Maginley made his first appearance in the ring at Shreveport, and made a hit as clown. The company consists of W. B. Carroll, Master Willie, Burdeau, Carr, Nayler Brothers, Bliss Family, P. H. Seaman and Cary, clowns; Billy Manning, Harry Blood, Alex. Prentice, John Somers, Master Hubert, Master Jimmy, W. A. Johnson, Mlle. Marie, and Mrs. Carroll."[73]

At a March 7 date in Mobile, a benefit was given for the orphans of that city. One of the local papers was impressed with Barney Carroll's carrying act.

"An extraordinary feature was introduced, which astonished the natives. A sweet little female hunchey-punchey, only fifteen months old, performed the wonderful feat of riding in different postures on the head, shoulders and arms of her father. She seemed to enjoy it hugely. She was seated on his hand at one time, and held out at arm's length while the two horses galloped around at a lively speed. This act is the greatest ever witnessed in or out of the ring."[74]

---

73. New York *Clipper*, March 10, 1866, from a letter posted from Red River, February 15, 1866.

74. New York *Clipper*, March 24, 1866.

Haight took his agent, Doc C. S. T. Chambers, as partner to form an 1866 summer tour of Haight & Chambers Circus. The opening of a three-day stand at Atlanta on April 23 brought in a sum of $1,500. A correspondent from the show stated,

> "The representatives of Haight & Chambers' United Circus made their first grand procession in this place yesterday, creating a greater furor, if possible, than that of Sherman's, some time ago, the only difference being he taking the town by strategy, we by storm, for it did storm as if heaven and earth were at loggerheads.... The arena being lighted up with fluid, together with big, fat Ben Maginley's gas—the only legitimate son of Momus in the biz—disclosed to our gaze hundreds upon hundreds of the fair damsels of the Sunny South, together with the bone and sinew, making it a spectacle not often seen in this country."[75]

The company's roster was similar to the previous year's. The Carroll family was back, along with Maginley and wife, Marie. She still dazzled the audiences with her leap through a twenty-inch hoop, perhaps the only equestrienne in the country at this time to accomplish the feat. The Bliss family members were also repeats, Signor Bliss still exhibiting his ceiling walking skills. Alongside were Sam Rhinehart, ten-horse leaper and a somersaulter; Signor Farranta,

---

75. New York *Clipper*, May 5, 1866.

contortionist; William LaRue, general performer; Sam Lathrop, clown; William Naylor, rider; John Naylor, leaper and vaulter; Henry Burdeau and Carr, gymnasts and tumblers, and H. C. North, general performer. Master Charles Bliss ascended to the centerpole in the outdoor free act. Admission at this time was set at 75¢ and 50¢.

The sideshow, managed by Billy Manning, consisted of a minstrel troupe of Manning, Phil Diffenbach (minstrel show manager), Billy Sweetham, Eugene Gorman, George Powers, Corporal Max, Millie Louise (fancy dancer), Murray and Walters (clog dancers), McArthur, etc., a group of fourteen performers.

The firm got rid of its baggage stock in Atlanta and took to rail. It moved north into Illinois, Indiana, Michigan and Ohio in April, reportedly doing good business. Louisville, Kentucky, was played for three days on May 7, 8, and 9, which, in spite of poor weather, seemed to have been profitable. "The pressure of other duties kept us from making but a very brief stay under the canvas," the man from the *Daily Courier* explained after visiting the opening, "but we saw enough to satisfy us that this is the best circus that has yet visited our city." He was most pleased with the performances of Marie and Ben Maginley. Noting that the canvas was full, he expressed a desire to see the complete show at another time. And indeed he did.

> "Notwithstanding the unpleasant walking last night, a large audience of both ladies and gentlemen were gathered at the circus. The

quiet, order, and commendable absence of all rowdyism and vulgarity, speaks volumes of praise for the management, while the unexcelled performances by the meritorious corps of artists testify to their liberality and good taste."[76]

Two days in Indianapolis followed, May 18-19. Then there were stops in Maryland and Virginia. Baltimore was visited for a week beginning August 30 at the Belair lot. The opening performance was well received by the *American and Commercial Advertiser*.

"This organization, depending solely on the merit of its performances, and not upon what is usually termed *gulling* the public, with a combined menagerie and circus, the menagerie consisting of nothing more than an exhibition of a few *antiquated fossils* in the form of lions, &c., has met with a proper and just success."[77]

Washington, D. C., was booked for three days beginning on September 6. At Charlotteville, Virginia, where the show appeared on September 18, the company visited the grave of Job Foster, who had died while with Robinson & Eldred in 1851, and performed a respectful remembrance at the site.

A correspondent, writing from Oglethorp, Georgia,

---

76. Louisville (KY) *Daily Courier*, May 8 and 9, 1866.

77. Baltimore (MD) *American and Commercial Advertiser*, September 3, 1866.

on October 15 claimed that the show was doing well through Tennessee and Georgia. There was a two-day stand at Atlanta on October 9 and 10, which packed their 115-foot canvas. A correspondent writing on October 28 confirmed that the show had been "meeting with unbounded success, the spacious canvas being crowded upon each occasion to overflowing."[78]

The company went down the Alabama River from Montgomery to Selma, where they had a two-day stand on October 29 and 30, and were expected at Vicksburg, Mississippi, about November 20. Harry Tibbs, scenic rider and juggler on horseback was added to the company about this time.

Haight then returned to Texas. A visit to Houston was successful. "The business with this company is represented as having never been excelled in that state," so read a *Clipper* item. "The circus, we are told, closed doors every night during the week beginning December 6, being unable to accommodate the multitudes." But in two weeks from that date the company had left the state and had arrived in New Orleans for a series of performances at Front Levee Street beginning on December 18. It moved further up town for the 30th and continued there through January 6, after which the show broke up for the season.

The *Clipper* reported that there were eighteen circus organizations on the road in 1866, a year which did not equal the financial success of the previous one. Most of them did good business during the first four months,

---

78. New York *Clipper*, December 22, 1866.

but in August and September all felt the pressure of hard times and an inordinate amount of rainy weather exacerbated the situation. The forecast for 1867 was not promising; and, indeed, for Haight & Chambers the season became a series of misfortunes.

The two proprietors purchased the stern wheeler *Coosa* in February 1867 for $30,000 and fitted it up expressly for circus use. They also arranged for ten cages of animals from Ames' Circus, which included performing cats under the whip of Ames' wife, Signora Ella Eugenia DeLorme. A *Clipper* item stated that the show carried fifty horses, 130 people and a 180 foot round top. That had to be a crowded boat.

Advertisements read, "The Largest and Best Show Traveling"; "Everything New! Everything Gorgeous! Forty-Nine Lady and Gentlemen Performers, Three Humorous and Witty Clowns"; and in the South, "The Only Southern Equestrian Confederation in Existence."

In the administrative department, Andrew Haight was manager; Dr. C. S. T. Chambers, agent; Fred Bailey, advertiser; O. B. Fowler, writer; Jacob Haight, Andrew's brother, treasurer; Herr Lengel, in charge of the animals; Tom Poland, equestrian director; and Prof. Stovey, musical director of a thirteen member band. Tom Fey was the boss canvasman, with Pete Garvey joining shortly as his assistant.

The performing roster was headed by English and Parisian equestrienne Marie Macarte, one of the first females to attain stardom in the United States; but who, at this point, was in her early forties. Supporting her and the "Lion Queen" were the Miaco Brothers, William Naylor, Sam Lathrop, Tom Burgess, Sam Rhinehart, Henrico Tubbs with his horse Stonewall, etc. Miss Jennie Day made a daily outside ascension at 1 P.M., following the "grand procession."

George Conklin, the long time animal trainer, then a lad out of Ripley, Ohio, joined a circus for the first time with this show. He began working in advance with agent Frederick H. Bailey. His job was billing towns and announcing the coming of the circus at market places, blacksmith shops, courthouses, and assembling a crowd by ringing a bell. He recalled in his memoirs that a show bill was about a yard square, containing a few woodcuts and printed matter. One placed at a livery stable sufficed, it being the only safe spot where the youngsters would not tear it down. Bills were not pasted up at that time, rather fastened to a wall with tacks driven through small rounds of leather. Conklin worked about three days ahead of the show, riding on horses hired from livery stables, but returned every three or four days for instructions and supplies.

The pattern of travel was to stop at the larger settlements going up the river and then visit the places that had been skipped over on the way back down. Conklin estimated the attendance at each being from 2,500 to 3,000 people. Residents of the smaller places nearby were brought to the performances by free boat excursions. It was a good-sized circus for those days, George Conklin wrote, with eighteen or twenty performers and thirty-five or forty working men.[79]

The show started from New Orleans on March 14 and worked up the Mississippi to Memphis where a four-day stand beginning April 3 was rewarded with a good turnout. "One of the largest and most delightful audiences we ever remember having seen at any place of amusement was present last night at the inaugural exhibition of Messrs. Haight & Chambers Circus and Menagerie," so wrote a man from the *Daily Appeal*. "There can be no question that this is one of the most attractive and complete exhibitions that has ever visited the city, and one that all can feel a pleasure in witnessing." He judged the performance of Ella Eugenie in the dens of lions and bears to be "the most remarkable instances of female courage and daring ever witnessed." It rained the second day, yet the animal exhibitions from 10 A.M. to 12, and the afternoon and night performances were crowded on each occasion to the utmost capacity of the canvas.

It appears that Herr Lengel alternated in the den performances with Ella Eugenie. The *Daily Appeal* reporter had praise for him in an April 6 item. "It is well known that the 'monarchs of the forest' are fiercer at some seasons of the year than others. Those now on exhibition here are so violent that the ordinary performer does not approach them, but Herr Lengel entered the den yesterday and subdued in a manner that we have never seen equaled." At the closing performance a foot race competition was arranged between

---

79. George Conklin, *The Ways of the Circus*, pp. 2-3.

representatives of the various Memphis fire companies, the prize being a silver drinking set. Company No. 2 was the winner, with fireman Phalen circling the ring ten times in a minute and eleven seconds.[80]

The show continued up river to Cairo, Illinois, for an April 9 engagement, after which it made a turn into the Ohio with intentions to go as far as Pittsburgh. But flooding interfered with the planned itinerary and forced the show to miss many of its dates, with some places being ten to fifteen feet under water. Evansville, Indiana, was safe for an April 15 visit, where the canvas on both occasions was filled, with hundreds being unable to obtain admission.

But that night a most unfortunate incident occurred. Some prankster opened the valve of the ship's boiler, allowing all of the water to escape. When the fireman lit up in preparation for moving on, the boiler was burned to ruin. Unable to continue the tour, the company pitched their tent again on the Evansville lot and peddled a few dodgers around town to alert the public of their unexpected return. The boiler problem required the show to perform two more days there.

The *Coosa* was then towed to Henderson, Kentucky. Although the town had not been previously advertised, dodgers passed around were sufficient to encourage a satisfactory turnout. On April 20 the show was at Owensboro, Kentucky, after having been advertised to appear there on the 17th. And thus, it continued on, three days behind schedule while two new boilers

---

80. Memphis (TN) *Daily Appeal*, April 4, 6 and 7, 1867.

were arranged to be installed. It got as far up the Ohio as Steubenville for a June 4 stand, then turned back for three days at Cincinnati beginning on the 10th.

By July the *Coosa* had left the Ohio and was back moving up the Mississippi. It docked at Davenport, Iowa, on the 16th, where a correspondent reported good business, afternoon and evening. At night the tent was filled to overflowing: "The leaping by the company was the best I have ever seen, led by young Sam Rhinehart, who performed on this occasion the feat of throwing a somersault over twelve horses, which was received with rounds of applause; he also accomplished the difficult feat of throwing a double somersault. Rhinehart is yet a young man, and if he continues to improve as he has since I last saw him, he will, without a doubt, soon have the right to claim the title of champion of the world. Mr. J. W. Naylor is also a good leaper, he having cleared nine horses on the same night. The principal act of horsemanship by Mr. William Naylor was excellent. The juggling on horseback by Harry Tibbs was well received. The double trapeze by the Miaco brothers took the house by storm. The 'Musket Drill' by H. C. Childers, was performed in a very artistic manner and took big. The horizontal bar by Charles Clouney, assisted by the Miaco brothers, was good. Signorita Ella Eugene, the 'Lion Queen,' was unable to appear, on account of illness. Report speaks very highly of this lady and her performing animals. On account of her not being able to appear, Herr Lengel, the 'Lion King,' who is with the company, kindly volunteered to enter the cage of African lions (three in number). Herr Lengel deserves a great deal of credit for the moral courage and daring manner in which he entered the cage of these animals and performed them. Old Sam Lathrop appeared at each performance, assisted by the Young American jester Billy Vershay. Sam cracked many a good joke, which the audience did not fail to appreciate. Billy appeared to good advantage, and managed to keep the audience in good humor. Mad. Marie Macarte is with the company, but has been very ill for the past two weeks, and unable to appear. I am pleased to learn, however, that the lady has so far recovered, it is thought, as to be able to resume her business again in a few days. Miss Jennie Day and Miss Libby Smith are also with the company, and appear at each performance in their different roles. The brass and string band connected with the company is under the direction of Prof. Storey. Mr. Thomas Poland is master of the arena and equestrian director."[81]

There was a week in late August at St. Louis to fair business. But cholera broke out on board the ship at

---

81. New York *Clipper*, July 27, 1867.

East St. Louis. Then, after going the short distance up river to Alton, Illinois, one of the cooks died. On the return two canvasmen also died. A short time later, two deck hands were smuggled off the boat. In early morning the clog and wench dancer, Johnny Lewis, came down sick and was removed to the Everett House in St. Louis where by five o'clock he was dead. The room was sealed until midnight when city officials removed and buried him.

Finally, local health people tagged the boat and sent it into quarantine. This dilemma lasted but a half hour before Haight fixed it with a couple hundred dollars and received a certificate of clearance. But the matter didn't end there. According to the *Clipper*, nearly the whole company quit. John and William Naylor and Sam Rhinehart left to join the Carroll & Maginley circus at Indianapolis; Ella Eugenia, the lady lion tamer, Mme. Macarte and Sam Lathrop went ashore at St. Louis; and Billy Manning joined Van Amburgh's menagerie.[82] On the other hand, later ads list the names of Rhinehart, Lathrop, Naylor, and Ella Eugenie, so we assume there was confusion in the *Clipper's* reportage. Mme. Macarte, Billy Manning and John Naylor are the only absentees. The Holland Family was added to the roster just before Haight & Chambers left the St. Louis area for St. Joseph.[83]

In September the show was received at river towns

---

82. New York *Clipper*, September 4, 1867.

83. Also listed in September were Henrico Tubbs, Tom Poland, Samuel Hinds, Gus Shaw, Tom Burgess, Jennie and Nellie Day, Mattie McCall, Miaco Brothers, H. Bernard.

along the Missouri. The Atchinson, Kansas, *Daily Champion* of September 21 pronounced it the "best exhibition of the kind that has visited us for a long time." It added, "After the humbug 'Yankee Robinson' perpetrated, we are glad to record the fact that one show, at least, is not a swindle."

By October 7 the show had returned down the Mississippi to Memphis for three days, the 7th 8th and 9th, again setting up on the Union Street lot, between Third and DeSoto. At this time the admission prices had risen to $1 and 50¢. The Memphis engagement was followed by going up the Red River to Shreveport and then into Texas by wagon. The company arrived at Galveston on November 27 for six days. The *Daily News* lamented its parting with, "Every effort is used to secure the pleasure and comfort of the people who attend, and it will be a sad day to hundreds of our young Americans when Doc Chambers pulls up stakes, packs his dromedary, mounts his elephant and wends his way to other climes."[84]

After a four-day stand at Houston beginning December 3, the troupe continued on through Texas, crossing as far as San Antonio for the week of December 25. But, finally, it went to grief at Houston on January 19, 1868, and the property was attached by the sheriff for unpaid expenses. It has been said that the season's disasters resulted in a $75,000 deficit, with Andrew Haight, the principal owner, being the major loser. With this, the Haight & Chambers partnership

---

84. Galveston (TX) *Daily News*, December 3, 1867.

dissolved.

Charges of embezzlement of about $60,000 were made in the Justices' Court of Harris County, Houston, against Andrew and Jacob Haight by Doc Chambers. Jacob, being the treasurer of Haight & Chambers, was arrested and held in confinement. Andrew was said to have absconded and carried the missing funds with him. The warrant claimed that payments to cover salaries, transportation and other expenses were issued through bogus drafts on a Galveston bank after the funds there had been withdrawn, thereby leaving the employees bereft of their earnings and their creditors empty-handed. Jacob was also exposed as being an expert in short changing at the ticket window.[85] The situation, with one partner on the road in advance of the show and the other partner's brother serving as treasurer, was left wide open for trouble.

Nothing came of Chambers' claims, perhaps because Haight had taken such a heavy loss on the season and Chambers being only a minority interest holder. So Chambers left to go on the Colonel Ames show as general agent, taking the animals with him. The outfit, which was quite a large one for the time, having been built up from a 115-foot round top to a 180, with good

---

85. From a letter to Frank Queen, dated Houston, Texas, January 19, 1868, carried in the New York *Clipper* of February 15, 1868. Conover's version is somewhat different, but unfortunately there is no citation. According to him, following the closing at Houston,"[Haight] had, however, taken the precaution beforehand to send his brother, Jacob Haight, north with what money there was (rumored to have been $60,000) so that there would be little for his partner, the performers, or the working men to attach when he did not pay off." Conover, *The Circus, Wisconsin's Unique Heritage*, p. 13.

stock and equipment, was sold and Haight went to Memphis, where he opened a hotel for the balance of the year.

The *Coosa* was sold to John Robinson, who used it to tow his circus for a season. She was then purchased by a private party from Cincinnati who ran moonlight excursions and similar events. Finally, as if still burdened by the Haight & Chambers curse, she was burned to the water's edge in the Licking River by an arsonist on the morning of September 7, 1869.

Andrew Haight was more interested in controlling the fate of his circus by making decisions as an agent in advance than by daily remaining on the lot. After all, he had his brother to see to his financial interests there. So he spent the two seasons ahead of the Stone & Murray Circus, a high class company that had no menagerie, but always carried a fine stud of horses and ponies. The two proprietors, very intelligent and capable circus men, were more concerned with quality than quantity. Here Haight perfected his skills in advance of this company for the seasons of 1869 and 1870.

He became noted for driving a close bargain and rarely getting the worst of it. Proprietor Murray was quoted as saying, "If there is any fault in Andy Haight, he is too close a contractor." This persuasive ability earned for him the sobriquet of "Slippery Elm." A peculiarity was his wearing clothes in the fashion of a clergyman. Press agent Charles H. Day described a first meeting with him in a railroad office. "The railway official was in close communication with a clerical individual whom I at once took for the pastor of a local church arranging for a Sunday school excursion. He was dressed in solemn black, wore a vest buttoned to his throat, and displayed no jewelry, while meekness and piety seemed to ooze from every pore of his placid countenance."[86]

A similar misidentification occurred when Haight was in St. John, New Brunswick, with his Empire City Circus. Upon meeting the mayor, he bowed ceremoniously and said, "Your Honor, we are coming to be with you for a little while and I have called to consult you in regards to license."

"Not necessary, sir," the mayor replied hastily, "you are at perfect liberty to preach without a license."

Haight was back in management for the 1871 season. He bought two performing dens of wild animals from the late C. T. Ames estate (Ames died on November 2, 1870), acquired some camels, and organized the Empire City Circus with P. Bowles Wooten, a mule dealer from Atlanta, for 1871. It was also referred to as Wooten and Haight's New York Circus and Menagerie.

The early season roster included equestrians Mlle. Ellouise LeClaire and Ella Stokes; Mlle. Andrews and Mlle. Louise, rope-walkers; Barney Carroll, with Master Willie and Petite Annie; the Watson Brothers, Edwin, George and Thomas; the lion queen Mlle. Minnie Williams, assisted by W. B. Reynolds; clowns Signor Bliss, Jean Johnson and Billy Andrews; J. C.

---

[86]. Charles H. Day, "With Tights and Spangles," New York *Clipper*, July 13, 1872.

Long, hercules and light and heavy balancer; and Jerome Tuttle, double somersaulter. There was Herr Kopp's Silver Cornet Band that paraded the streets in the "Oriental Chariot of Oberoe" drawn by twelve Arabian horses. W. W. Durand was the general agent, and A. R. Scott, the contracting agent. George DeHaven and Jacob Haight had the privileges. Prof. Renno made daily ascensions in his hot air balloon.

The circus opened its doors to the public at Duluth, Georgia, on April 1 and then headed north, covering an area that included Ohio, Pennsylvania, and New York State. At Jamestown, New York, there was a day and date with Sheldenburger & Co.'s Menagerie and Circus (a John V. O'Brien concern). Both parties advertised extensively and developed a rivalry that created a strong anticipation for their arrival. Being a railroad show, Haight did not make much of an entrance; but the Sheldenburgers, a wagon show, were said to have "come in strong," with cages gaily ornamented, new uniforms on their band members and drivers and colorful flags unfurled. "This captivated the people and both afternoon and night their pavilion was crowded."[87] In June the show was in the New England states, going as far north as Maine. Following dates in Calais on July 3 and 4, it went into Canada for the rest of the summer months, where business was reported good.

Following the incursion of the provinces, Haight and Wooten's company went through reorganization in Boston beginning September 9. New wardrobe and

---

87. New York *Clipper*, May 27, 1871.

paraphernalia were acquired, as well as a 125 foot tent with a "cottage front," all in preparation for a southern tour.

The outfit was loaded onto the steamer *Seminole*, under Capt. Matthews, which set a course for Savannah, Georgia, arriving at 8:00 P.M. on September 14. "She had a full freight and a large list of passengers, among which was Wooten & Haight's Circus Company, eighty performers, and a large number of horses, cages, &c."[88] As the boat steamed up the river, the spectators ashore were serenaded by Herr Kopp's brass band in anticipation of Haight and Wooten's return to Georgia after a year's absence.

The show had reentered a part of the country where the citizenry were enthusiastic to claim it as their own.

> "This circus was organized in Atlanta, Ga., in 1870, and it is a purely Southern affair, which of itself should be a recommendation from it to our people. Both the managers are natives of Atlanta, and well known in that section, while the performers are, in the majority, Southern men.... Taken as a whole, we suppose that this circus can lay just claims to being the most complete and extensive one now on exhibition, and as our people are cognizant of the fact that it is not a *Yankee humbug*, but a legitimate and deserving institution composed of men who, although engaged in what is generally conceded to be a 'Yankee calling,' are

---

88. Savannah (GA) *Morning News*, September 7 and 15, 1871.

Southern in sentiment. We bespeak for the circus a liberal patronage while in the city."[89]

This was a two-day stand, but because of a late arrival the previous day, the first performance was delayed until the evening of the 15th. At 5:00 P.M. the show's aeronaut made his balloon ascension and Harry Wambold walked the wire from the ground to the center-pole and back. You can bet the sideshow was up and running and the concession stands ready to serve the crowd who came to see the free attractions. "Persons of all grades, sex and variety gathered to witness the grand event of a genuine balloon going up, and a real live man going in it."[90]

A balloon ascension as a circus free act, as we have indicated, was initiated in 1870. Although lighter than air vessels had been exhibited in this country since the late eighteenth century and were used sparingly during the Civil War, they were a novelty in most places circuses visited. The Savannah *Morning News'* description of such an event illustrates the excitement caused by the phenomenon:

> "At the appointed hour the balloon was detached, and with its cargo of one man went sailing up into the air, while the band struck up the merry peals of 'Up In The Balloon, Boys.' The cheering was immense. Those who never cheered before now opened their lungs the

---

89. Savannah (GA) *Morning News*, September 7, 1871.
90. Savannah (GA) *Morning News*, September 16, 1871.

more, and away went the daring aeronaut gaily plowing the air above.

"When the balloon arose it took a northwesterly course over the city, and when somewhere near the vicinity of the Exchange, it began rapidly to descend. The people on the streets seeing that it would inevitably fall in the river, a general rush was made for the Exchange dock. When directly over Bay street, the man in the balloon divested himself of his coat, hat and boots, and, it would seem, was ready for the splash that he and his cloth vessel in a few minutes made in the middle of the river. When he fell, he was soon pulled on board a boat, and, with the exception of getting a ducking, escaped unhurt.

"When the man came on shore, there was something less than seventy-five thousand people on the wharf, who exhibited the wildest excitement. Men halloed, women shrieked, little boys shouted, boot blacks whistled, chimney sweeps screamed, and dogs barked, the whole making one grand hullabaloo, which would forcibly remind one of a flock of ten thousand geese invaded by a mean looking hound dog.

"The man was escorted by about a thousand interested people to his boarding house, when the crowd dispersed, each one to tell his experience of what he knows about the balloon."

This auspicious welcome extended to the opening performance. "Not within the recollection of the oldest inhabitant has so large a crowd been collected within a circus tent as was attracted last night to welcome Messrs. Haight & Wooten's troupe of equestrians. For an hour previous to the beginning of the performance, the streets were lined with one surging mass of humanity, so that by 8 o'clock the capacious pavilion was filled to overflowing, several hundreds being compelled to retire unable to gain admission."[91]

The show moved to Augusta for the 19th and 20th onto a lot near the Augusta Hotel, where it received a similar reception. "Not withstanding the very heavy rains, the performances were attended by large crowds. The exhibition came fully up to what was expected, and gave entire satisfaction to all who were present."[92] This day the valiant aeronaut experienced a near miss of repeating a plunge into the Savannah River, landing as he did on its bank. Unfavorable weather persisted into the second day; but, in spite of it, attendance was large, so wrote the *Daily Chronicle and Sentinel* of September 21. "The company has made a very favorable impression during its short stay in our city, and will be substantially remembered on its next visit."

Atlanta was a successful three-day stand on September 28, 29 and 30. This was confirmed by a post-opening report.

---

91. *Ibid.*

92. Augusta (GA) *Daily Chronicle and Sentinel*, September 20, 1871.

"Yesterday afternoon and evening the streets presented a gay and animated appearance. Upon Mr. Haight placing a piece of cardboard in our hand, we passed into the spacious and excellent pavilion in the rear of James block, and above the passenger depot, and found out what was the matter with Hannah and every other man, for everything was crowded—not a seat, a standing place, or even a pole could be found to hang on. It is estimated that over three thousand were present. We could not realize that this magnificent enterprise had grown to such an extent in so short a space."[93]

Although the Chattahoochee River beckoned, our aeronaut steered clear of it. This time, with the floating balloon showing frequent signs of collapsing, the professor landed safely on the roof of a building on the corner of Fraser and Rawson Streets.

P. Bowles Wooten was gone early in November. The proprietors did not agree and the show, by common consent, was auctioned off, Haight buying most of the property, DeHaven the rest. The circus now traveled under the name of Haight & Co. Wooten acquired animals from someone; for but two months after his departure from Haight & Wooten he was out with Wooten & Andrews' Great Southern Menagerie and Callisthenic Exposition, moving around Georgia.

A frightening incident occurred as the company was preparing to leave Amite City, Mississippi, for New

---

93. Atlanta (GA) *Constitution*, September 29, 1871.

Orleans on November 16. A group of about twenty-five men on horses set upon them as they were boarding the train. Two shots were fired, one hit a camel in the side and the other pierced a passenger car that contained the women and children. The men in the company left the train and were able to capture two of the raiders, who were then taken to New Orleans and placed in the lock-up.[94]

The C. T. Ames collection of animals was auctioned off at the Rink in Cincinnati on the 14th of November. Haight & Co., which had acquired a new tent for their menagerie in late October, claimed to have purchased a part of it, greatly extending the size of the animal exhibit. "The Management, at an enormous expense, has purchased the entire and complete Menagerie of the late Colonel C. T. Ames which in conjunction with their own makes the largest and most splendid collection of Zoological wonders in the world, embracing SIXTEEN MASSIVE DENS OF LIVING WILD ANIMALS."[95] This claim runs contrary to an item published in the *Clipper*, which listed the purchases and the buyers of the Ames collection. Neither Haight nor DeHaven were included.[96] Nevertheless, advertisements listed a monster elephant, Bismark, and a baby elephant, Pet, in addition to hyenas, a sloth, a cheetah, two dens of lions, tigers and panthers, a lioness with six two-month old cubs, monkeys and birds.

Charleston's January 18 and 19 appearances are

---

94. New York *Clipper*, December 2, 1871.

95. Advertisement, Charleston (SC) *Daily Courier*, January 9, 1872.

96. New York *Clipper*, November 25, 1871.

further examples of the company's success. It arrived there by way of the Savannah and Charleston Railroad and set up on the Citadel Green, from which the usual balloon ascension took place. By now the aeronaut was a Mr. Garbood. This time the man landed precariously upon a shed of the Ann Street depot of the South Carolina Railroad.

> "In the evening there was an immense attendance of ladies and gentlemen, who witnessed the startling feats of grand and lofty tumbling, equestrianism, and the gymnasium, with evident delight. The whole program was carried out to the letter, and in a manner that establishes this company as one of the most perfect traveling organizations of the kind we have ever seen. The menagerie is well supplied with the wonders of the forest. The side shows contain a Swiss warbler, a dwarf, a magician, whose tricks are unfathomable."[97]

The long season was terminated on February 17 in Atlanta. The outfit was then moved to Cincinnati, where it was combined with other elements to form the 1872 tour of the Great Eastern Circus.

The first indication of organizing the Great Eastern appeared in the New York *Clipper* of February 10, 1872. "Messrs. DeHaven and Haight were in Cincinnati last week, arranging to start from there with a menagerie about the middle of April. They are having the

---

97. Charleston (SC) *Daily Courier*, January 19, 1872.

wagons made in Porkopolis. R. E. J. Miles, the well known manager, has engaged to travel with them." These three men, with the connection of past associations, would assemble a circus out of the remains of the former Col. C. T. Ames' Menagerie, Agnes Lake's Hippo-Olympiad, and Haight's Empire City Circus that was to experience a highly successful season through brazenly exaggerated advertising and an aggressively combative policy toward all rivals.

THE GREAT EASTERN CIRCUS OF 1872
A FANTASTICAL JOURNEY

The Great Eastern was set float in the dawn era of modern circuses, when, in 1871, the Barnum organization established a new standard of operation. The size and expense of this first-year circus was far beyond anything offered in the past—three large exhibition tents, separating the menagerie, the museum, and the arena, between five and eight horse tents holding about thirty head of baggage stock each, a total spread of canvas covering nearly three acres. The show moved in ninety-five to one hundred wagons. At the outset, the main tent seated some 5,000 people, but by the end of April, it had been expanded to accommodate over 7,000. The cost of operation was unprecedented in the circus business, with daily expenditures amounting to as much as $2,500. P. T. Barnum's Great Traveling Museum, Menagerie, Caravan and Hippodrome was in a league by itself.

In 1872, the outfit designated the "Greatest Show on Earth," an advertising slogan used for the first time that season, had grown to such proportions that it necessitated a move to rail travel. There were ten tents on the lot, and three ticket wagons, one of which was reserved for ladies (women's suffrage being a hot issue); and they were kept busy.

Adam Forepaugh's circus was also a contender for public acclaim by 1872. His menagerie was the best on the road, with its some thirty cages of animals, a pair of elephants and seven camels. In addition, of course, the daunting presence of Adam himself was an intimidating force. Forepaugh and Barnum, both generous with their spread of lithos and their use of multi-column newspaper displays, presented awaiting competition for the newly formed Great Eastern.

The idea for the Great Eastern probably originated with DeHaven while in the advance of Agnes Lake's Circus during the winter of 1870-1871. DeHaven, a man of big dreams, once said to agent Charley Pell, "Any man can start a circus with money, the thing of it is to put one on the road without any." He contended that powerful publicity, lavish advertising and good people in advance could keep a circus running; and, as the money came in, it could be built up along the way. Andrew Haight was the perfect man in advance and R. E. J. Miles, as a theatrical promoter, was experienced in financial matters. These three men put the Great Eastern on course.

The Great Eastern Menagerie, Museum, Aviary, Circus and Balloon Show was announced to debut at the Exposition Building in Cincinnati on March 25. Instead, it opened at the National Theatre on April 1, the site where R. E. J. Miles had been the lessee for the years 1868-1870. Because there was not room in the building for the menagerie, the animals were placed in the street as a gratuitous exhibition. The circus remained for a week, giving matinees daily.

In the *Clipper's* early season announcement, the proprietors were Dan Carpenter, R. E. J. Miles, George W. DeHaven and Andrew Haight. Carpenter, who was the treasurer, may have initially put up some money, but soon disappeared from the management roster. A. R. Scott was the advertising agent; Jacob Haight, was also listed as treasurer; W. Scott, program agent; Barney Carroll, equestrian director; and Francis S. Koppe, leader of the band and co-proprietor of the sideshow with Ben S. Potter. Capt. Breese controlled the candy privilege.

W. W. Durand, the general business agent, is attributed to a large share of the show's success. Charles H. Day described him as "a typical Southerner, who smoked like a chimney and chewed plug tobacco and wrote with the sledgehammer of conviction."[98]

The procession took the normal pattern, led by a bandwagon and followed by cage vans, all interspersed with people on horseback, the elephant Bismark, camels, etc. An advertised feature was Herr Elijah Lengel's wild cats "loose in the streets." Actually, Lengel sat atop a cage wagon, beneath a canopy, accompanied by a lion, two leopards and a dog.[99] A calliope drawn by a

---

98. Day, "Happy Days at the St. Charles."

99. Clinton (IA) *Age*, July 3, 1872.

dozen horses, belching steam and blaring out a racket, brought up the rear.

The Great Eastern was the only circus to make use of a calliope with the show this season; and, indeed, the only circus since 1860. Calliopes were used on the riverboats, but for people removed from the water routes it was still an object of astonishment, one that created both excitement and derision from the public and the press. Fred Dahlinger, Jr., in his research on calliopes, found no real description of this particular one and no indication of its source.[100] The Racine (WI) *Advocate* expressed a sardonic opinion of the instrument, which we include here in its entirety:

> "Descend, O muse, and give us befitting language in which to describe that fearful and wonderful machine which goes under the classical name of Calliope—we confess that we are not equal to the task. Our vocabulary of superlatives is not large enough to give the reader the slightest idea of our opinion of it. From descriptions of the machine, we had acquired a sort of vague idea that it was a huge organ, whose seraphic strains would put to shame any music, which we had ever heard; under who's gentle but powerful influence the tigers became harmless as doves and the lions lay down with the lamb. You may judge then our feelings when we heard the machine go off

---

100. Notes made by Fred Dahlinger, Jr., for a more extensive piece on calliopes.

for the first time. Our impression was that a fire had broken out and that all the whistles in town were going at once; but when we found out what it was, our disgust was too deep for utterance. A choir of Tom cats or shanghai roosters would furnish music which would be angelic harmony when compared with the Calliope. We have heard it said that it sounds better at a distance; we presume this is so, and the greater the distance the better."[101]

The museum consisted of Gen. Littlefinger, "the smallest man in the world"; a fat woman; Prof. Owens, magician; Signor Ghio, warbler; a tank of Alaskan seals; and various curiosities. Not comparable to Barnum's exhibits, but what else was?

The ring performance was surprisingly strong for an infant organization, indeed, easily competitive with both Barnum's and Forepaugh's. Agnes and Emma Lake were there, as were the Carroll family—Madame and Barney, Master Willie and Annie and Dolly Varden. In addition, there were Mme. Cornelia, equestrienne; riders Charles H. Lowry and Fred Sylvester; gymnasts Thomas V. Watson, Jean Zacco and the Miaco Brothers; leapers, Jerome Tuttle and Adolph Gonzales; clowns Billy Andrews, P. H. Seaman, Lee Fowler and Tony Ashton. Robert Ellis introduced the elephant Bismark; Herr Lengel performed with a den of lions, tigers and panthers. The champion leaper George M. Kelly was added later in the month.

---

101. Racine (WI) *Advocate*, June 1, 1872.

After a week in Cincinnati, the show moved into Kentucky. The *Clipper* reported the night's receipts at Lexington were $2,200; the matinee at Frankfort, $1,100. Louisville followed on Friday and Saturday, April 13 and 14, with the outfit set up on the corner of Fourth and Chestnut Streets. A pre-arrival announcement lauded the advance advertising. "The gorgeous posters and extensive presentation of the many features of the circus and menagerie have attracted much curiosity, and no doubt an excellent business will be done in this city."[102] Kentucky dates continued through May 1, after which the show moved into Indiana, Illinois and Wisconsin.

The circus arrived late at Evansville on the 2nd, and did not get ready for business until nearly three o'clock. Both the parade and the balloon ascension were omitted. In spite of this, attendance for both performances was sizable. The *Daily Journal* of May 3 reported that "The animal collection is not as large as we were led to believe it would be, but it is still very interesting, particularly the young lions, the young elephant and the camels; but there is still room for more, considering the exhibition is 'twelve shows in one'."

A seven day stand in Chicago was split between the West Side, on the corner of Madison and Elizabeth Streets (May 15-18); and the South Side, on the corner of State and Twenty-second Streets (May 20-22). We remind the reader that the great Chicago fire was but

---

102. Louisville (KY) *Courier-Journal*, April 13, 1872.

seven months past, ignited on that fateful Sunday evening at 9 o'clock of October 8, 1871. The inferno, abetted by a strong wind out of the southwest created a devastated district encompassing an area four miles long and, on average, three-quarters of a mile wide, laying siege to some eighteen thousand buildings and causing a total of two hundred million dollars of damage. One hundred thousand people on the North and East Sides of the city lost their homes and an untold number of work places. One might expect that the unfortunate citizens of Chicago were not ready for circus entertainment; but that would prove wrong.

The Great Eastern ads indicated four mammoth pavilions, covering three acres of ground, with a menagerie of twenty-six dens of wild animals, carpeted seats for the women, and the great elephant Bismark. "In consequence of the magnitude of the exhibition and the Herculean labor to be performed in order to get ready for an afternoon performance May 15, a grand street display will not take place on Wednesday." However, there would be the gratuitous balloon ascension and the exhibition of the musical calliope each day at 2 P.M.[103]

The receipts of the matinee on this opening day were quoted at something over $1,700. As for the evening: "If the fact that over 7,500 persons were in attendance argues anything for the popularity of the establishment, there can be no doubting its success. The actual amount taken in at the door last evening

---

103. Chicago (IL) *Tribune*, May 10, 1872.

was $8,003.50."[104]

In truth, the crowd was so immense on the lot for opening night that the canvases were not large enough to accommodate all of it. The *Tribune* stated that it was "by far the largest crowd ever assembled beneath a canvas in Chicago, if not in the world." The estimate was 6,000 people.

> "The jam at last became so dense and irresistible that the ring ropes were broken in, and the charmed circle was given over to a struggling mass of humanity. The performers were fairly crowded out, and retired to the dressing-rooms, leaving the ring in the possession of the audience. A dozen policemen proved powerless to restore order; the band essayed some soothing strains to no purpose; the clown exhausted his wit and his indignation without avail; and at last, *dernier ressort*, the elephant was brought in and trotted ferociously around the ring, but as fast as the ungainly brute cleared a space the crowd ran in behind him, so that the only good he accomplished was to stir up matters, very much as one stirs up punch with a spoon by keeping it moving round and round."

The elephant was finally led away, and it was not until a large number of people left the pavilion that the performance was allowed to continue. Even so, only a

---

104. Chicago (IL) *Inter-Ocean*, May 16, 1872.

portion of the program was given.[105]

The Great Eastern's move to the South Side appears to have maintained the established momentum. "Here there was quite as great a rush to it as was experienced on the other side of the river. The large tent last night was crowded to the full, and the performances were received with unbounded satisfaction." On the Wednesday afternoon, a benefit showing was given for the Orphan Asylum, under the patronage of Gen. Sherman, the Mayor of Elgin and the people involved in the management of the place.[106]

We might add here that another circus establishment opened in Chicago at this time on a lot in the unburned west side of the city, on Clinton Street, between Washington and Randolph, "Nixon's Parisian Hippodrome and Chicago Amphitheatre." The front of the edifice presented an attractive appearance with gas jets extending the entire length and an elegant arch over the entrance. The interior was arranged with chairs in tiers from the ring to the canvas top and a commodious promenade was adorned by panels elaborately illustrated with scenes from the sports and pastimes of former years, rendered by the well-known Chicago artist R. W. Wallis. The place was lighted with gas, thoroughly ventilated, and could comfortably accommodate 2,500 people. Admission to the building was 50¢ for the parquet and dress circle, 75¢ for reserved chairs, and 25¢ for children under ten. "There was a

---

105. *Ibid.*

106. Chicago (IL) *Inter-Ocean*, May 21, 1872.

very large crowd in attendance upon the initial performance," the *Inter-Ocean* reported, "large enough to test the strength of the house, the hasty construction of which had raised some doubts as to its safety. The performances were not of a very novel character, but good of their kind, and those of the audience who were able to endure the suffocating atmosphere of the interior ought to have been pretty well satisfied."[107]

The Great Eastern spent the month of June in Wisconsin and Minnesota for the most part. According to the *City Times*, performances at Janesville on the 3rd were well attended. The parade began around ten o'clock. "There were a number of beautifully painted cages containing animals, on top of one of which Mr. Lengel the lion tamer was seated, caressing a large Bengal tiger and a leopard, which did not act in a very leopardly manner; two camels and a microscopic elephant also took part in the procession, which was closed by the wonderful calliope, a sort of a cross between a steam whistle and a hand organ, and which proved highly attractive to the small fry." The paper also made note of the "accompanying number of side shows, spring guns, etc., where considerable money was wasted."

The circus came to Fon du Lac on the 4th in, according to the *Daily Commonwealth* man, twenty-five freight cars. And in his judgment, "The Great Eastern comes as being near what it advertises to be as almost any that comes to Wisconsin. There is

---

107. *Ibid.*

a large crowd in attendance, and will be a still larger one tonight."[108] At Columbus, WI, on June 9 the town was jammed with people visiting the place, with an afternoon house of about $1,000.[109] A comment in the Watertown *Republican* of June 12 noted, "It is fair to assume the street display hardly came up to general expectations, several things in the bills being minus in the procession."

Four immense tents were advertised for the La Crosse date of June 13. The *Daily Republican and Leader* announced the following day that the show "brought together the largest number of people ever seen in one body in this city." The afternoon performance was said to have had a ticket sale of $2,500, or 5,000 customers; the night attendance a 1,000 fewer. The performances were considered first-rate, and the reporter "had no hesitation in saying the 'Great Eastern' is a number one show and deserving of patronage wherever it goes." It appears that Herr Lengel received injuries while at Portage City, so his turn was eliminated for the date.[110] St. Paul played host to the circus on June 17 and 18, Minneapolis followed on the 20th. The *Daily Tribune* was unapologetic in its praise. "Unquestionably the Great Eastern Circus, Menagerie, Aviary and Balloon Show is one of the greatest exhibitions on the road. Their caravan, as it paraded the streets yesterday, formed an imposing sight. The procession must have been a mile long, and the whole concern in all its appointments is

---

108. Fon du Lac (WI) *Daily Commonwealth*, June 4, 1872.

109. Beaver Dam (WI) *Argus*, June 12, 1872.

110. La Crosse (WI) *Republican and Leader*, June 14, 1872.

first class. Both afternoon and evening the tents were crowded and every one came away delighted."[111] Iowa, Missouri and Illinois were visited in July. At Clinton, the *Age* writer commented that the show came "nearer filling the bill advertised than circuses usually do." He was satisfied with the menagerie—"Of course this part of the show attracted many who would not otherwise have attended." The arenic performance was similar to circuses generally, but the Carroll family stood out. "Master Carroll who is but thirteen years old, secured applause repeatedly and he earned it in every case. He turned somersaults backwards several times in succession while his horse was on the gallop. He is surely an equestrian wonder."[112]

At Burlington on the 11th, a local review of the Great Eastern was as glowing as many before it.

> "All Burlington, most of Des Moines County, and two-thirds of Western Illinois, were in town, yesterday, gazing with delighted eyes upon the gorgeous pageantry of the circus. From dewing morn until high twelve, the happy people thronged the business streets, or sought with panting eagerness the shady corners…. At eleven o'clock, the lookers out for the grand cavalcade heralded its approach. They saw it on its winding way, and were happy…. The band and the Oriental Monarch among his tigers and leopards were 'the cynosure of all

---

111. Minneapolis (MN) *Daily Tribune*, June 21, 1872.

112. Clinton (IA) *Age*, July 3, 1872.

eyes' until the calliope and its attendant host appeared. The Dromedaries and the baby elephant and the buffalo calf were warmly welcomed. The music of the steam whistle was enchanting. It did not excite much enthusiasm, however—owing probably to the fact that we have a great deal of it at home."

Burlington being on the river, the citizens were familiar with the steam organs on many of the passing boats. The crowds here were immense; filling what the writer termed "the three-fold" tents. The circus tent, in particular, was jammed.[113]

The citizens of Keokuk lined the streets "on the tip-toe of expectation" during the morning of the 13th. The *Gate City* observed that the procession came and went and was merely a repetition of what had been seen before. The calliope, however, was deserving of mention. "The particular novelty was a steam musical institution on wheels, which screeched and blowed much like the screeching and blowing heard every hour on the Levee." The paper noted that the circus required thirty-three cars to transport it from Fort Madison to Keokuk.[114] The circus visited St. Louis for five days beginning July 22. Here we see for the first time in the St. Louis *Democrat* of July 20 the claim of "The Six Great Tent Show," not four as had previously been in the advertisements. The ads also read, "DOUBLE CIRCUS RING. Two performances in separate pavil-

---

113. Burlington (IA) *Gazette*, July 12, 1872.
114. Keokuk (IA) *Gate City*, July 14, 1872.

ions at the same time, by the first talent of Europe and America. Two grand orchestras and a steam piano." Earlier ads of the 13th and 14th were still using the "Four Immense Pavilions" claim. It is possible that former cuts and text inserts were still in use; or can it be that at some point in July of 1872, perhaps at this St. Louis stand, the Great Eastern became the first two-ring American circus? Not likely.

The pre-announcement in the St. Louis *Times* reflected the usual advertising boasts. "The mammoth combination will spread its canvas, comprising six large tents, tomorrow on the lots extending from Eighth to Eleventh on Spruce streets. The show includes twenty-six dens of wild animals, with elephants, camels, a museum of startling wonders and a full double circus company. The grand entrée will be made on Monday morning, headed by three brass and reed bands and a large martial band, and our citizens will have an opportunity of seeing tigers, panthers and lions marching along loose in the streets. A really good show like this cannot fail to do an immense business."[115] A day after the fact the *Democrat* acknowledged that a large crowd had filled the streets, "attracted by the gorgeous parade which was enlivened by three bands of music, a steam calliope, a cloud of banners, squadrons of prancing horses, and a number of wild beasts." The opening night audience was "almost uncontrollably large," according to the paper. "It surged back and forward like a great sea, rippling waves against the walls of tents, coursing

---

115. St. Louis (MO) *Times*, July 21, 1872.

irresistibly through the passage ways that connected the different apartments and drifting about in the wide hippodromes." The writer was pleased with the selection of the performers, which was confirmed by "the constant storms of applause." However, not once did he mention two rings in separate tents giving simultaneous performances.[116]

A bit of excitement occurred on the morning of the 23rd at the Southern Hotel. Herr Lengel entered the lobby with his pet leopard and reached the cigar stand before the animal arose and put its front paws on the counter, sending cigar boxes tumbling about. Lengel restrained the animal and calmly led it through the rotunda, a wide path being made by the spectators, and into the bar where he proceeded to consume an order of soft-shelled crabs. After which, he led the leopard out. No three-column ad was needed to publicize the circus on this day.[117]

There was rain that evening, but it had little effect on diminishing the attendance. The *Democrat* reported, "The series of tents were thronged again, and the brilliant exhibitions in the arena were loudly applauded." Notice it did not say "arenas," thereby adding to the dilemma of two rings. As the performance neared its

---

116. St. Louis (MO) *Democrat*, July 23, 1872. The parade went from the circus lot up Seventh Street to Franklin Avenue to Twentieth Street, up Twentieth to O'Fallon to Broadway, down Broadway to Fourth, down Fourth past French Market to Carondelet Avenue, down Carondelet to Russell Avenue, Russell to Union Park, up Decatur Street to Park, down Park Street to Ninth, up Ninth to Hickory, Hickory to Seventh, Seventh to Spruce and to the lot.

117. St. Louis (MO) *Democrat*, July 24, 1872.

close, the gasoline lights suspended on the center pole caught the rigging on fire, threatening to ignite the tent. Fortunately, the rain had saturated the canvas, making it fire resistant. The lights were pulled down and the blaze was doused with water. Meanwhile the crowd scattered in every direction, to the exits and under the sidewall, all screaming and yelling. The management eventually calmed the disorder, put up new lights and the performance continued to its end.[118] The *Democrat* of the 26th gave a final note in summary of the week's stay. "The exhibitions have been alike profitable to the public and to the managers, the latter having reaped a harvest from the immense throngs that have been constantly in attendance. Among the many attractions during the week have been the performances of Miss Emma Lake, who has a very winning face and is an exceedingly graceful and dashing equestrienne."

The stand at Belleville, Illinois, on July 27, encountered a ticket-selling problem. A young man buying two seats for the matinee claimed he gave the seller a five-dollar bill and received no change in return. Getting no satisfaction from the seller, the man went to the office of the Justice of the Peace, from which he received a writ of attachment. At the end of the evening performance, an officer named Seifort, bent on attaching one of the horses, went to the circus grounds, where workers taking down the tent set upon him. They beat him fiercely, pummeling him from one side of the ring to the other, like some low rated heavyweight. Seifort

---

118. *Ibid.*

was able to draw a revolver, but before he could use it the piece was knocked from his hands. In the scuffle, he was hit on the head with a large wooden stake, which crushed his skull. He was taken home in an unconscious state, from which he never recovered.[119] For the Edwardsville date of July 29, the ad read, "One Ticket Admits You to the Six Tents"; but again, no mention of a double company and simultaneous performances.

The Great Eastern spent the month of August in Illinois, Indiana, Ohio and Pennsylvania. A two-day stand at Cleveland opened on the West Side of the city at the corner of Detroit and Oakland Streets on August 20 to large crowds for both afternoon and evening performances. On the 21st, the company moved across to the East Side at the corner of Superior and Dodge Streets, where there were three performances given. The *Herald* indicated that the one at 10 A.M. was "for the special benefit of ladies and children, who by going at that hour will avoid the crowds of the afternoon and evening." At the night show a number of the troupe were unable to perform due to illness caused by the excessive heat.[120]

The show exhibited at Union Park, Allegheny City, PA, on the 23rd to what the Pittsburgh *Post* called immense audiences. "The performances and curiosities are well worth seeing. The balloon ascension was a success and was witnessed by a large crowd of spectators." On the 24th, the long train of wagons and vans

---

119. New York *Clipper*, August 10, 1872.

120. Cleveland (OH) *Herald*, August 21 and 22, 1872.

crossed the river, passed through the principal streets of Pittsburgh, set up on a lot at Penn and Thirty-first Streets and again performed to good business. From the correspondent to the *Clipper* we learn that one ticket was good for the museum, menagerie and the circus, "three separate tents" and that the menagerie count was fifteen cages.[121] However, the advertising in the Cleveland *Herald* and the Pittsburgh *Post* still exaggerated a "Six Tent Show" and "the largest collection of animals in the United States." The Great Eastern started into the South with the beginning of September and remained in the southern states until closing in mid-December. It visited Augusta for September 12, and still claimed to be a six-tent outfit with three performances a day, but no indication of a double ring.

At Charleston, SC, for the 13th and 14th, the *Daily Courier* writer was astonished at the riding of an infant.

> "Charleston has had the honor for the past two days of seeing, perhaps, the youngest and tiniest Knight of the Sawdust that ever bestrode a horse or won the plaudits of an audience. Master Dolly Varden Carroll, who belongs to the Great Eastern Circus, is a prodigy of such juvenile proportions as has never yet appeared before the public. On Saturday, when he made his appearance in the ring, amid a grand flourish from the band, there was heard a murmur of astonishment and bewilderment from the female portion of the audience. Imagine an

---
121. New York *Clipper*, September 7, 1872.

infant of about three summers, two feet four inches in height, and of about twenty pounds weight, trotting into the ring, and approaching a double team of horses, with the avowed intention of performing equestrian feats on their backs, and you will have an idea of Master Dolly Varden Carroll's appearance."[122]

Earlier in the century, there was a public clamoring to watch children enact adult roles in the theatres of both England and America. We do not refer to the Elizabethan child actors who were trained to perform women in a company of adult males, for in Shakespeare's day they functioned within the established conventions of sixteenth-century theatre; whereas the nineteenth-century infant prodigy performed a repertory of difficult roles, usually requiring a mature virility, alongside a company of adults, and was made "to hector, and combat, and conquer what he could hardly reach."

Master William Henry West Betty, the most celebrated child actor of the nineteenth century, a boy of thirteen years when he became the rage of London, charmed the theatre-going public into a temporary loss of rationality and engendered a national enthusiasm. His brief but flamboyant career opened the way for innumerable sucklings with such whimsical titles as Infant Columbine, Infant Clown, Infant Hercules and Infant Vestris. As late as 1851, Barnum in America and Europe was promoting the Bateman Sisters (Kate and

---

122. Charleston (SC) *Daily Courier*, September 16, 1872.

Ellen). The girls, six and eight years of age, performed Shakespearean scenes and farce afterpieces.[123] The circus was not immune from using infant prodigies as feature attractions, usually apprentices, with names fronted by "Master" so-and-so or "Young" so-and-so, and the younger the better for audience appeal. In 1836, Thomas Taplin Cooke brought his stable of child performers to this country, a troupe of precocious youngsters, astride ponies, flailing into combat, creating a romantic illusion that particularly pleased the female section of the audience.[124]

According to the Charleston *Daily Courier*, Dolly was born in New York State in November of 1868, making him three years, ten months old. Mr. and Mrs. M. B. Carroll were his parents. Further,

> "...At the mature age of eleven months Master Dolly first began life on his own account by

---

123. On May 16, 1805, less than a month after Betty completed his first successful season, Master Mori, the Young Orphius, performed a concerto on the violin at Covent Garden. A short time later, Master Wigley, a four year old, executed several pieces of military music on the bugle horn at Drury Lane. That same year, the Belfast theatre company was augmented by the appearance of Miss Mudie, an eight year old, hailed as the female Betty. A young actor, billed as the American Roscius, John Howard Payne, made his first appearance on the stage as Norval in 1809. In 1817 the six year old American, Miss Clara Fisher, was introduced at Drury Lane. Five year old Master Joseph Burke, the Irish Roscius, was an instant favorite at the Theatre Royal, Dublin, in 1824. Called the "greatest musical and dramatic wonder of the age," the versatile Burke played the violin, sang Irish tunes, led the orchestra in the overture and enacted both comedy and tragedy.

124. There was also a trout named Dolly Varden, olive green with orange or red spots, growing two or three feet long and weighing from five to twelve pounds, native to the streams of the Pacific Northwest of the United States, Canada, and Alaska.

discarding the creeping process of locomotion and attempting to move about on his own pedal extremities. In these attempts, his success was so marked that he was urged to undergo a course of training for a profession he had selected. Accordingly when he had reached the age of three years and a half he was put upon horseback, under the tuition of his father, and after two or three months of training, in which he suffered several narrow escapes from such trifling accidents as being trodden under the horses feet, or having his brains dashed out, Master Dolly made his first appearance in public. He has been acting now just about three weeks, and in a conversation with a reporter of the *Courier* on Saturday, expressed his great liking for the profession. He further stated that as yet his performance consisted only of riding around the ring, standing on his father's pericranium, but he professed great confidence in his ability to ride by himself, and stated that he intended to do so as soon as 'papa' would let him."

Three summers old, indeed. Dolly Varden was either a dwarf or midget, a ward of Barney Carroll's, performing in the guise of a perennial toddler. The reader will remember the earlier carrying act of Carroll's with little Willie, who now, a few years later, is apparently too heavy for such acrobatics, and, therefore, is being replaced by an eternally small substitute.

We might suggest that Dolly's was an adopted name inspired by the original "Dolly Varden," a type of female attire, a gaily-printed muslin dress popular from 1865 to 1870.[125]

The Great Eastern arrived at Charleston by way of the South Carolina Railroad on September 13 and took possession of the Citadel Green lot. There was no matinee given on that day, but its place was taken by the street procession, which attracted a sizable curbside crowd. As described in the *Daily Courier*, the spectacle was headed by a handsome bandwagon; following up was Herr Lengel atop one of the cages with his pet feline performers and a line of other cages, each confining a wild beast of some sort, which could be only partially seen through the air holes on the sides. And, of course, there was the impatiently anticipated steam calliope, "whose music was loud enough to be heard squares off." Bringing up the rear were the single elephant, some camels and other animals on the hoof.

The evening performance accommodated the largest and most respectable audience since the war. There were indeed six pavilions, all arranged so that each exhibition led comfortably to another and could be easily viewed at one's leisure. The main canvas was brilliantly lighted by gas manufactured on the spot, which created a pleasing effect upon the gold and silver banners over the arena and enriched the colorful costumes of the performers as they went through their

---

125. Charleston (SC) *Daily Courier*, September 14, 1872.

paces.

The man from the *Courier* expressed satisfaction with the performances. "The acting was excellent throughout, and in some instances extra fine. The startling trapeze performance; the riding, and especially by the little girl and infant boy; the grand and lofty tumbling, all were better than we have witnessed in years."[126] At Savannah, for September 17 and 18, the six tents were advertised and, in a September 14 ad, a double-ring. Again, there were to be three performances daily, as a "Grand Moral Matinee" for 10 A.M. was added. However, because the circus train arrived late, only the evening performance was given on the first day. In spite of the inclement weather, the company played to standing room and turn away business. Yet, no confirmation of a double ring.

Haight's shows have always been popular in Georgia, and this year was no exception. The Savannah *Morning News* led its story on the following day with, "This colossal amusement institution—decidedly the largest arenic and zoological display ever in this section—had an immense house last night." The writer, heavily influenced by the handouts of the press agent, judged the menagerie to be "complete and meritorious," containing "every rare animal to be found in the jungles of Bengal, the wilds of Africa, the hot sand deserts of the East and the palace-pens of Egypt." Continuing: "The collection of birds, monkeys, etc., is complete, and cannot fail to at once attract the attention

---

126. Savannah *Morning News*, September 18, 1872.

of lovers of ornithology and the Darwin theory. Every parent who desires his children schooled in this branch of moral instruction, should not fail to avail himself of this most excellent opportunity to give the little ones a lesson. This tent being entirely separate and distant from the arenic performance gives those who desire to see the menagerie alone, without being compelled to witness the circus, such a rare chance as they will not soon have again."[127] Here we can see the influence of the southern charm of press agent Durand.

Gold stars were awarded to Annie and Willie Carroll, Barney Carroll and Dolly Varden, the horizontal bar act of Tony Ashton, and the hurdle riding of Charles Lowry. Since we last listed the roster of performers, we find new additions that include the Runnell Brothers, hat spinners; A. P. Durand, general performer; and William Painter, gymnast and acrobat. However, there was still no comment from the local press about the simultaneous performances. In viewing the single ring, at least, the parting item of the 19th included, "The tumbling was good, the posturing excellent, the trapeze act thrilling… But we didn't see the six tents or the ten lady riders."[128] At last, someone took the trouble to count.

Another item on the 19th suggested grift. "As usual, at all large gatherings, there was a fair sprinkling of the light-fingered gentry at the circus on Tuesday night, who had an eye to business. We are informed

---

127. Savannah (GA) *Morning News*, September 19, 1872.

128. Undated item from the Thomasville *Times*, repeated in the Savannah (GA) *Morning News*, November 12, 1872.

that a lady in passing from one tent to another, had her pocket picked of her portmonaie (sic) containing sixteen dollars. Why people should go in to such crowds with any amount of money on their persons is a mystery that we cannot now explain." As it happened inside the facility, it suggests that someone paid for a profitable privilege.

At Thomasville on the 25th, the parade appeared limited because of threatening weather, so the *Times* reported. "The train of animals, cages, band wagons, and last, but not least, their celebrated steam piano made up the show.... Outside of this they did not attempt any street display, except the daring feat of a man riding on top of a wagon with three loose tigers." The calliope belched "Up in a Balloon, Boys" as it passed down Broad Street.[129] This sounds like the usual lineup, the weather being a good excuse for a procession much less than a mile in length.

When Atlanta was visited on October 5, the Atlanta press wrote all the right things as usual. Noting that the circus raised its "six tents" and that the natives were all charmed by the spectacle, the *Constitution* continued with, "The Great Eastern, by its bills, promised a great deal, and its performances filled the bills. Andrew Haight is along, and Haight never travels with, or gets up any other but a first class show. The artists are all first-class, the clowns witty, the horses in fine condition and well trained, the animals in good order and

---

129. Atlanta (GA) *Constitution*, October 6, 1872.

full of life."[130] The *Sun* reported that, "Not less than 8,000 persons, of all ages and all classes, witnessed the arenic, hippodramatic, and zoological exhibition of this magnificent combination last night. Such an assemblage of people was probably never seen in Atlanta; and among them were about 4,000 women, who came, the highest and the lowest, to see the grand medley performance by sixty skillful professionals, and the magnificent array in the zoological department." It confirmed that three entire pavilions were devoted to the menagerie—monkeys, baboons, panthers, leopards, lions, bears, wolves, hyenas, camels, deer, moose, buffalo, elephants, ponies, and a number of birds. "One of the most wonderful, if not the most wonderful features of this combination is the little boy rider, Dolly Varden Carroll. A little boy, to all appearance not more than two years of age, balances himself on the head of one of the equestrians, and rides around the ring at a fearful speed. Altogether this circus and menagerie is one of the most remarkable combinations before the public."[131]

The Great Eastern continued in Georgia, Florida, Louisiana, Mississippi, Tennessee and Alabama during the remainder of the tour. At Pensacola for October 19, the ad clearly stated, "Double Circus Troupe, and Double Circus Performances Given in Separate Tents at the Same Time." However, for the Mobile dates of October 21 and 22 we found no evidence of this double

---

130. Atlanta (GA) *Sun*, October 6, 1872.

131. Mobile (Ala.) *Daily Register*, October 22, 23, 1872.

performance.

The circus arrived at Mobile on a Sunday evening, and was fresh and ready for the street procession the following morning, which elicited a positive reaction from the local press. Calling it a "stupendous affair," the *Daily Register* of the 22nd expressed pleasure at "the long line of wagons, filled with trained animals, the camels and elephant turned loose in the street, the brass band and calliope, all proving that the Great Eastern was certainly a big thing on wheels." After viewing the menagerie and the arenic performance, the writer conceded, "that the herald of the Great Eastern had not exaggerated its proportions or its excellence."

Reportage on the 23rd was equally positive:

> "This circus and menagerie, the most extensive which has visited us, folded its tents and went away last night, after affording our people much amusement and lining the pockets of the enterprising managers with greenbacks. At each performance, the six tents were crowded fully, rather uncomfortably so in fact, by all classes of people, who expressed their unqualified delight at the manner in which they were entertained, the arenic performance being far superior to that usually found in the generality of circuses. Take it all in all, the mammoth show, including the fine collection of animals, is the best, in all its departments, which we have seen in this part of the country and we can safely hand over the Great Eastern,

and its polite managers and agents, to the favorable notice of our brothers of the quill in other places."[132]

The season ended at Selma, Alabama, on December 13, 1872, with the two-ring claim still in question. The show traveled a total of 9,404 miles and netted a large profit. Sturtevant gave the figure at $100,000, George Hall, Jr., at $350,000, and W. W. Durand at $424,000.[133] The correct amount may lie somewhere in the middle.

We have found no evidence of there being simultaneous circus performances. How could this have been accomplished? Two performances occurring in separate tents at the same time, with conflicting noises of band and audience? In addition, how was it done with a performing roster that was seemingly the same as at the start of the season?

No contemporary writer has bothered to inform us. John A. Dingess, who was an agent for the show during the latter part of the season, wrote in his unpublished manuscript that DeHaven conceived the idea of the second ring. "Not two rings, wherein inferior performances were given, 'as is the custom nowadays,' but two separate tents, with equestrian performances in each, at one and the same time." Unfortunately, that is the extent of his explanation.

The Great Eastern's chief rival, P. T. Barnum's

---

132. Sturtevant, *The White Tops*, January, 1929; Hall, *Billboard*, June 24, 1922; Durand, *Great Eastern Advance Herald*, 1873.

133. *Courier*, January 19, 1873.

Great Traveling World's Fair, was using "Six Separate Colossal Tents" this year and had frequently included the line in its advertising: "The first and only show in the world that uses a double circus ring, and requires a double circus troupe of performers." Actually, the second ring was formed by the increased space between the ring and the audience, created by the use of a larger canvas pavilion to accommodate an extended seating area. This space, which formed a ring around the ring, was for circuses the origin of what we now refer to as the hippodrome track. Therefore, the true explanation for the advertisements of two rings in 1872 is that there was a new performing area around the single ring that was used for greater spectacle.

The Barnum show followed the Great Eastern into St. Louis by a week. With such competition so close, the Great Eastern adversary usurped the Barnum advertisements by claiming six tents and a second ring of their own. That is the only explanation possible.

The initial year of the Great Eastern ended to unusual financial success, thanks to the shrewd management team and the immense amount of advertising, both factual and fantasy, that was posted. With money in their pockets, the trio of owners split, DeHaven and Miles joining Spencer Q. Stokes in taking out the Great Chicago Show, and leaving Haight to pilot the Great Eastern for 1873.

THE NOT-SO-GREAT TRANS-ATLANTIC CIRCUS AND MENAGERIE

Pardon A. Older (1826-1908) was a wagon show manager who traveled chiefly in the Midwest. He is reputed to have traded a sawmill at Janesville, Wisconsin, worth $5,000, for a third interest in the E. F. and J. Mabie circus in 1849. The show had about seventy horses, eight wagons, an eighty-five-foot round-top, and a thirty-foot dressing tent. Older's Great U.S. Circus followed this in 1852. Others under his name included Orton & Older's, with Miles Orton in the years 1858-60, and Older's Museum, Circus and Menagerie, 1870-72.[134]

Agent John Dingess, who was with Older's 1873 organization, described him as "one of the most gentlemanly of managers," recalling that he was "extremely popular in every section of the country, especially throughout the West," and in appearance being easily taken for a person of the clergy.[135]

At the end of P. T. Barnum's 1872 season, a smaller

---

134. William L. Slout, *Olympians of the Sawdust Circle*, p. 227.

135. The Dingess unpublished manuscript.

show was formed in Detroit and sent South under the management of P. A. Older, leased to use Barnum's name and partially financed by him. There was a suggestion that Coup was opposed to the splitting up of the animals and equipment, but Barnum was interested in promoting his name in the South. He could not do it with his own large show because, with his rail car wheels built for the northern "standard gauge" tracks (four feet, eight and one-half inches in width), it would be too expensive, time consuming and cumbersome for them to be changed to accommodate the "southern gauge" (five feet in width), still in use throughout much of the South. The deal appeared to be a good one for both parties; the Barnum name was expected to draw large crowds and the surplus animals loaned to Older would be cared for throughout the winter months.[136]

The tour opened in Louisville, Kentucky, on November 4, 1872, and then followed a route through Kentucky, Tennessee, Georgia and Louisiana, ending up with financial trouble in New Orleans. An eight-day stand there closed the operation, which was said to have lost Older his life's savings of $60,000.

Old John Robinson "owned the South." Circuses under his name had covered the territory for years. In opposition to Older, his press department flooded the route in advance with bills and couriers using Barnum's literature, but attaching it to the Robinson show title. When the Barnum advertising was posted, the Southerners rejected it with "that Yankee clock

---

136. William L. Slout, *A Royal Coupling*, p. 53.

peddler has copied Uncle John's bills word for word." The magical name of "P. T. Barnum" had not appealed to Southern audiences.

In December, Barnum went to New Orleans to reclaim the property. In his autobiography, he makes no disclosure of the Older show's failure, but simply states that he was in New Orleans visiting his Southern show. At this time, some of the animals were sent back north. Richard E. Conover wrote that Coup was also there at the time. This was confirmed by an item in the New York *Clipper*—both Barnum and Coup went to New Orleans "to look after the interests of Barnum's Southern Museum, Circus and Menagerie."[137]

C. G. Sturtevant, quite the contrary, alleged that Coup refused to go. We believe Conover's entry to be correct.

On January 23, Older and J. M. Chandler contracted to buy the show property from Barnum & Co. that had been stored at Algiers, Louisiana, following the termination of Older's lease in December. Chandler had been Older's general agent for the doomed winter tour. Because of the planned enlargement of the Barnum show, this was probably redundant equipment. So here, P. T. made another of his close deals. The purchase price was $50,000 plus a "rent" of seven percent per annum. An advance of $5,000 was given the proprietors to get started. Older could draw up to $6,000 in salary, Chandler up to $2,000, and they were allowed to keep $2,000 on hand for emergencies. All profits were

---

137. P. T. Barnum, *Struggles and Triumphs*, p. 683.

to be returned daily to the Barnum company in New York. Older and Chandler were required to guarantee funds necessary to provide winter storage, replacing of animals, and re-fitting of the show in the event the debt was not paid in full by the end of the season. Barnum & Co. retained the privilege of placing a man on the show if so desired at the expense of Older & Chandler. The name of P. T. Barnum was not to be used in any way (Louis E. Cooke claimed that it was). Barnum & Co. retained the right of repossessing the rhinoceros for $7,000 if the one they had in New York died before the start of the season. The contract was signed by S. H. Hurd, treasurer, P. T. Barnum & Co., and by P. A. Older and J. M. Chandler.[138]

The deal gave Older re-birth in circus management under the title of Older & Chandler's Trans-Atlantic Circus and Menagerie. The tour took the show from winter quarters at Algiers into Mississippi and, from there, north into Indiana, Illinois, Kansas, Missouri, Iowa, Minnesota, Wisconsin, back down to Kansas and, ultimately, Texas.

Although show advertisements proclaimed greatness—the largest and best show on earth, a menagerie of 500 living wild animals, a monster black rhinoceros weighing two tons, a white elephant, an aquarium of sea monsters, sea lions, seals and two monster crocodiles twenty feet long from the river Nile, 100 star performers, seven colossal tents on five acres of ground, a magnificent procession two miles long, and

---

138. Richard E. Conover notes, obtained by photostatic copy in the possession of Tom Parkinson.

the tent brilliantly lighted by 5,000 gas jets—it was a comparatively small show with a weak company. There was a promise of free daily balloon ascensions made by Sig. Figaro, "the great Spanish balloonist" in his "monster balloon Madrid," and performances in double rings, all for the standard 50¢ and 25¢.

We see, from the advertisements, at least, that Barnum's automatons "The Sleeping Beauty," "Bell Ringers" and "The Dying Zouave" were exhibited, as well as Fiji Cannibals of some description. The featured performers were Mlle. Watson, equestrienne; W. H. Taylor, hurdle rider; the Victorelle Family (Marie, Antoinette, Oscar and Little Victor); and a man named Chapman (perhaps with trained horses).

The show tangled early in the tour at Evansville, Indiana, with the Great Eastern, which was scheduled to visit there on April 12. The Trans-Atlantic preceded it by appearing on the 4th, out-advertising it in the press and equaling it in exaggerated claims of size and excellence. The Great Eastern was scheduled to appear at Belleville, Illinois, on April 14, with the Trans-Atlantic arriving ahead on the 9th. There was no comment from the local papers, so we are at a loss to judge the success of either; but we know from the newspaper advertisements they both made bold promises that neither were equipped to carry out.

The Topeka *Daily Commonwealth* of May 2 reported:

> "Topeka was yesterday bowed down under a disappointment as bitter and an affliction as heavy as the hog cholera or the horse disease.

A circus came to town and it rained like a second deluge, making a very tame and wet affair, and washing the paint off the automatons, causing them to look like miniature mummies without their Sunday clothes on. The procession passed through the principal streets at the usual hour, the ponies and goats sinking almost out of sight in the mud, which, to use a sweet comparison, was of the consistency of good sorghum molasses. In the afternoon, a performance was given to a fair crowd, composed mostly of Kaws [local Indians] and country folks, the stormy weather preventing the residents of the city from attending. In the evening, the attendance was what might be called good. It was different in that respect from the show."[139]

At Chetopa, Kansas, the show butted heads with George W. DeHaven's Great Chicago, starring James Robinson. The Trans-Atlantic was booked for July 18; the Great Chicago for August 9. The *Southern Kansas Advance* was not compassionate in its observance:

> "The 'Great Atlantic-Exposition' has come and gone. Two of Chetopa's lots, not remarkable for their dimensions, only were required for their 'seven colossal tents.' Their gas had all evaporated; consequently, their balloon would

---

139. Orin C. King, "Only Big Show Coming," *Bandwagon*, September/October, 1987, p. 22.

not go up. The 'magnificent procession,' two miles long was condensed to about forty rods, with the wagons two or three rods apart. In the 'museum of 100,000 rare curiosities,' the chief curiosity was that ancient and dishonorable insect known as humbug. The '500 living animals' had nearly all died, and but few aside from a cage of very common monkeys were left. The monster black rhinoceros had escaped in Texas, and the sea monsters, sea lions, seals, crocodiles, slid out while they were being watered in the Gulf of Mexico. The greater part of the 100 star performers had deserted the outfit, and are staking out claims down in the Indian Territory. There was a town full of people to attend this tail end of a circus and menagerie, and we are sorry they did not get their money's worth after coming so far through the dust and dirt."[140]

Alas! After the Texas tour, the unfortunate circus folded in Shreveport, Louisiana. John Dingess, who was with the show at this time, recorded that the demise of the Great Trans-Atlantic occurred as follows: "After the tour of the state of Texas, and toward the end of the traveling season, the establishment arrived at Shreveport, La, where the performances of the company came to an abrupt termination by the appearance of yellow fever in its worst form. Everybody appeared panic stricken, and began to hasten away with

---
140. *Ibid.*, pp.22-23.

all possible speed; many, however, who were unable to get away, fell victims to the dread disease. All the performers and musicians, together with the writer and several other attaches, embarked at midnight on a steam packet bound for St. Louis, Mo., which was the last steamer to leave that port for many weeks.

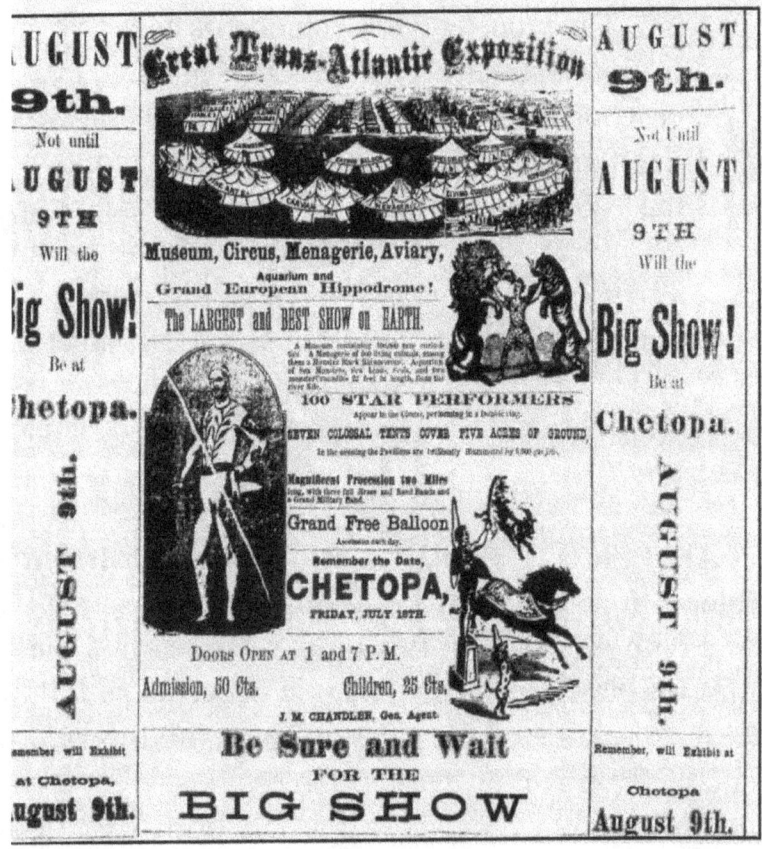

Many of the passengers seemed ill at ease until late in the afternoon of the following day, when the mouth of Red River was reached and were steaming up the current of the noble Mississippi, when perfect and real rejoicing began among all hands. The band played lively airs and selections from many of the most popular standard operas, and the inhabitants were regaled with choice music at almost every landing during the entire journey. The trip to St. Louis required some eight or nine days, when the people separated and departed in different directions to their respective homes. This was Mr. Older's last experience in show business."[141]

We thank Tom Parkinson and his search through the pages of the 1873 Shreveport *Times* for a more detailed reportage of the events.[142] The circus arrived at Shreveport on August 15 for a two-day stand, most likely on the circus lot at the corner of Milam and Edwards Streets. Rainy weather caused the loss of the matinee. The *Times* complimented John Barry's riding, along with first-class riding and tumbling in general. It also indicated there would be an additional performance on the 17th. "As the circus lays over until tomorrow, it will give a show tonight at the usual hour."

On the 20th, the ax fell:

> "COMES TO GRIEF. The Trans-Atlantic Exposition has been attached at the suit of several parties who belonged to the establishment. The employees have been thrown temporarily out of employment and out of means at the same time. To assist these men

---

141. Dingess manuscript, pp. 259-260.

142. Tom Parkinson, "Folding of Older & Chandler Show at Shreveport in 1873," *The White Tops*, July 8, 1949, pp. 3, 4.

a complimentary benefit was given them last night in which all the artists of the exposition assisted."

On August 23, the *Times* reported:

"The managers of the Trans-Atlantic Exposition have, so far as we can learn, honestly discharged all the obligations incurred here, which was done with the proceeds of the sale of their splendid horses—the finest, taken all together, we have seen in a circus. The animals have been attached and are now in the hands, metaphorically speaking, of Sheriff Flournoy, though this is done, if we are not misinformed, by some of the attaches of the concern. Indeed, a family disagreement seems to have been the origin on the financial troubles of the exposition. In case of the sale of the animals, we propose buying the elephant, rhinoceros, lions and tigers with which to guard our sanctum. They will do excellent service in lieu of the 'fighting editor'."

The circus people were exerting all efforts to raise traveling money. An ad on the 24th announced, "the artists of the Trans-Atlantic Exposition will give one of their attractive performances at Linman's Beer Garden today," the program including ring horses and the usual band, all for fifty cents.

The former Great Chicago, which had been bothersome in Kansas, arrived on the 30th, now billed as the Great James Robinson's Circus, Great Show of the South and American Exposition of Wonders, "the Greatest Show on Earth," featuring James Robinson, Frank Robbins, Mons. Duprat and sons, Robinson's sons, Clarence and Eugene, all riders; Leopold and Geraldine, acrobats; Stickney and King, clowns; the Royal Japanese troupe, and Prof. Judson's "flying ship of the air."

This same day the *Times* criticized the city administration for unsanitary conditions, causing a great deal of sickness. For example, city officials had not removed the carcasses of a hundred cattle, drowned when a steamer sank nearby. "If there is a city of the population of this in a civilized country that is filthier and that furnishes at every corner a greater variety of bad smells, we should like to hear of it."

By September 2, the dead cattle had been removed and the city had organized the Howard Association to fight illness. "Reports are exaggerated," the *Times* stated on September 3. "There is some yellow fever and there have been a number of deaths. But there is no epidemic." However, the ensuing death lists revealed the growing number of fever fatalities; and by September 14, they totaled 146. "Death is certainly making a fearful havoc with our citizens," the paper admitted.

An article, "THE CIRCUS AND THE PESTILENCE.," was placed in the *Times* on the 13th of September:

"The opinion has been growing in the community that the pestilence with which this city is afflicted was brought here from the vicinity of Mexico by the Trans-Atlantic circus, which broke up after its arrival among us, and the property of which is still camped in the heart of the city. The disease, which is so rapid in its course and fatal in its results, is pronounced by some to be a malignant type of yellow fever peculiar to Vera Cruz and that portion of Mexico. It is alleged that a number of the attaches of the Trans-Atlantic Exposition belonged to a circus that has recently been in that region; it is regarded as remarkable that a circus with the splendid paraphernalia and valuable properties of this one and belonging to so influential a capitalist as P. T. Barnum, should have broken up here for the want of money; it is affirmed that men connected with it abandoned it as an INFECTED show and not from pecuniary consideration, and it is stated with confidence that while the circus was exhibiting to our people there was a case of the present fever in the sideshows. Now these are serious facts and although it is too late to remedy the evil, still we think the properties of this circus should be removed from our midst. We believe that all the trunks, clothes and other articles capable of holding infectious poison should be burned up, no matter what their value, and that the animals and tents should be removed out of the city and there kept until disposed of. The animals should not be burned for they are harmless, except that they are, in a city, nuisances. We counsel the city authorities to consult the physicians of the city, and if the faculty approve these views, to act upon them FEARLESSLY and WITHOUT DELAY."

Forthwith, the animals were removed to the outskirts:

> "The authorities yesterday put their shoulders to the wheel and moved it, bag and baggage, and then fumigated the grounds formerly occupied by it. If nothing more results from it, the sick in the neighborhood will be relieved of the noise of the roaring of the lion and the howling of other beasts."

The circus was an easy target for blame, being foreign to the city; although no fingers were pointed in the direction of the James Robinson organization. In fairness, however, it must be mentioned that other possibilities were also voiced—the drowned cattle, decayed vegetable matter from the river that polluted the air; not to mention "electrical phenomenon beyond the comprehension of man."

The *Times* asserted that what many people believed to be Mexico *vomito* was introduced by employees of the Trans-Atlantic circus. "That it is the genuine yellow fever none can deny. That it was imported is very evident, and that, too, by the circus."

Everything belonging to the circus, save the animals, was auctioned off on the 20th, and a second sale was forthcoming:

> "State of Louisiana, Parish of Caddo, in the 10th Judicial District Court: Frank Stevens vs. Older & Chandler et al, William Porter vs. Older & Chandler et al, F. Watson vs. Older & Chandler at al, R. W. Fryer vs. Older & Chandler et al, John Barry vs. Older & Chandler et al.
>
> "In the Parish Court: J. L. Brooks vs. Older & Chandler et al, John Dingess vs. Older & Chandler et al, Charles Lewis vs. Older & Chandler et al.
>
> "By virtue of a writ of sale issued from the Honorable, the 10th Judicial District Court for the Parish of Caddo, and a writ of sale issued from the Honorable, the Parish Court of said parish in the above entitled suits and to me directed I will sell at public auction at the courthouse door in the city of Shreveport, parish and state aforesaid, on Saturday, Oct. 4, 1873, between the hours of 11 A.M. and 4 P.M. the following described property, to wit: 1 band wagon, 7 property wagons containing circus property, 1 wagon and cage containing monkeys and 1 kangaroo, 1 wagon and cage containing 1 deer and 1 peafowl, 1 wagon and

cage containing 2 lions, 1 wagon and cage containing 2 leopards and 1 hyena, 1 wagon and cage containing 1 rhinoceros, 1 wagon and cage containing 1 pelican and 1 black wolf, 1 wagon and cage containing birds and monkeys, 7 museum wagons and contents, 2 Goats, 1 Baby Elephant. All being the property attached as belonging to Older and Chandler and the Great Trans-Atlantic Exposition. Terms of sale—on a credit of 12 months, purchasers to give approved personal security. A. Flourney, Jr., Sheriff."

Six thousand people had fled the city. Deaths totaled 226. All stores were closed. "Shreveport is one great hospital." Sympathizers throughout the country sent donations, including P. T. Barnum, apparently no longer connected to Older & Chandler, who anted up $100. But the fever continued to rage.

On September 26, the newspaper abandoned the claim that the circus was to blame for the epidemic. "Few if any of the statements were substantiated." It asserted that the show had been made a scapegoat to protect Shreveport's reputation and its chances for expansion.

The sale of the animals occurred on October 4. A Mr. James Cumpston purchased the rhinoceros for $5,600, the baby elephant at $3,500, the leopard and hyena for $370, the lion and lioness for $555 and a cage of monkeys and birds for $202. Charles Frost bought the band and entrée horses.

Fever deaths reached 527 when the epidemic began to fall off; but final approval for the return of refugees was not given until November 5. It was determined by the committee of doctors that the epidemic had not been caused by the circus because it had come to town en route from Dallas and Houston, touching no infected point, leaving no trail of disease, with no member of its troupe sick on arrival. The conclusion was that the seeds of the epidemic had been brought from New Orleans on riverboats.

On December 18, the *Times* reported a show would be given under a pavilion at the usual circus lot—Milam and Edwards, the apparent remnants of Older & Chambers after its sale. Steven's Amphitheatre, as it was called, opened on the 23rd, with performances continuing daily through the holidays, under the management of Frank Stevens, the former treasurer for Older. Included in the programs were John Barry in his bareback act and Master Leon on the flying trapeze. A week later, it was announced that the show would give a free performance in appreciation to Shreveport on behalf of his enterprise. "This will be the last performance in this city for the present and Mr. Stevens takes this occasion to thank the citizens for their very kind offices to his companions who suffered from effects of the late epidemic."

In conclusion, the Trans-Atlantic was on the rocks before the yellow fever outbreak, not caused by it. Older was ruined again. Epitaphs appeared in the New York *Clipper* trade cards, advertising the sale of the Older

& Chandler property by John Caldwell of Shreveport and the animals by James Cumpston. Contrary to the assertion by Dingess, Pardon Older continued in show business for another decade before retiring to his farm near Onoka, Minnesota.

WHAT GOES UP... COMES DOWN
BALLOON ASCENSION FOR FUN AND PROFIT

The balloon ascension as a free exhibition to attract the public to American circuses was inaugurated in 1870. Previous to this, a pre-performance ballyhoo for many shows consisted of a parade through town, eventually ending up in front of the canvas pavilion. As the improvement of roads allowed circuses to travel with larger wagons and heavier equipment, parades became more elaborate and more spectacular. Band chariots, wagons exhibiting the contemporary lion kings and their beasts, huge and ornate pageantries on wheels, thirty and forty horse hitches, elephants and camels in harness, mechanical music rigs—all contributed at one time or another to the great advertising caravan.

During an age when every town had their own local band and a band stand was a symbol of pride in most every village park, band music on the circus lot was another means of attracting a crowd. Every show of reasonable size carried at least one group of uniformed musicians, the brass band being the loudest and thereby the most useful. In time, the musicians were augmented by mechanical devices. Spalding & Rogers brought out the Apollonicon in 1849, and Nixon & Kemp introduced the calliope in 1857, both oddities of their day capable of drawing avid public attention.

Another popular free act prior to the introduction of balloons was the daily ascension of a wire-walker from ground level to the tent's center pol. This device appears to have been inaugurated around 1856 when Sands' circus presented Mlle. Isabelle, who walked the wire a distance of some 300 feet. The following year there were at least five other shows exhibiting a similar act.[143] And not to be outdone, the creative Yankee Robinson featured the handsome young horse, Black Hawk, in 1857, trained to walk a plank on the perilous journey to the top of the tent, this according to Robert Dingess in his unpublished manuscript.

But at a time when airplanes were unheard of and the urge to emulate the magical flight of birds was a sometime youthful dream during the inevitable journey toward maturity, the phenomenon of a large balloon, filled with hot air, rising from the earth and carrying a man skyward was an awesome spectacle for people living in a horse-drawn century. And circus proprietors eventually came to understand this. The hot air balloon was first launched successfully in 1783 in France by the Montgolfier brothers. Their observation that smoke rose into the air was the basis for experimentation with

---

143. Polacsek, John F., "The Origin of the Extravaganza," in *Bandwagon*, November-December, 1973, pp. 28-30.

lighter than air craft. The original tests were naturally primitive. No passengers were sent aloft and the prototype did not achieve a great distance, but the theory was confirmed.

If at this early stage there were no logical uses for the balloon there was at least a curiosity value. Balloons became objects for exhibition and intrepid aeronauts the exhibitionists. On January 9, 1793, Jean Pierre Blanchard, one of the earliest of American aeronauts, ascended from the yard of the Walnut Street Prison in Philadelphia. President George Washington and an assemblage of dignitaries watched the hydrogen-filled balloon rise to over 5,000 feet and disappear in its travel of fifteen miles before alighting into a patch of woods near Woodbury, New Jersey. The craft carried Blanchard, his black dog, and a letter of introduction from the President—it being the first piece of air mail on the American continent. This was Blanchard's forty-fifth ascension but his first on our side of the Atlantic Ocean.

Blanchard, a native of France, had even at a young age an inventor's curiosity. As early as 1781 he constructed a flying machine fashioned after the manner of birds in flight, having four huge wings operated by hand and foot levers. The contraption was, of course, a failure. But once the Montgolfier brothers had proven the principle of lighter than air flight, Blanchard wasted no time in accepting the balloon as a legitimate device for exhibition and experimentation and in the ensuing years made forty-four flights throughout the European continent. His greatest triumph, however, eight years before coming to America, occurred when he crossed the English Channel with Dr. John Jeffries of Boston. This was the first air voyage between nations, hailed as "the eighth wonder of the world."[144]

The channel crossing occurred on January 7, 1785. It goes unexplained how Blanchard and Jeffries came to be partners in this historic event. Nevertheless, at 8:00 A.M. the balloon ascended over the white cliffs of Dover, a tribute to Blanchard's imagination. The gondola, shaped like a bathtub, had a rear fin and four wing-like rudders, attachments intended to steer and propel the balloon. Blanchard was seemingly unaware that the airship was solely subject to the whim and fancy of the wind and not human guidance. The flight, which was fraught with hair-raising events too lengthy to go into here, terminated shortly after three o'clock in the afternoon in a wooded area not far from Calais. The heroes of the treacherous crossing—unlike Lindbergh almost a century and a half later—landed inauspiciously, with no cheering well-wishers, no champagne, no flags unfurled.[145]

Returning to Philadelphia of 1793, one might wonder why anyone would choose to do anything within the walls of a prison. But to Blanchard, enclosure of the Walnut Street prison was essential for at least two reasons. It protected his equipment from

---

144. Blanchard, Jean Pierre, *The First Air Voyage in America*. Philadelphia: Penn Mutual Life Insurance Co., 1943, p. 10.

145. Stehling, Kurt R. and William Beller, *Skyhooks*. New York: Doubleday & Company, Inc., 1962, pp. 20-24.

mettlesome curiosity seekers and it allowed him to charge an admission fee for observing the preparation and take-off of his balloon. Then, too, the open space of the prison yard was free of encumbering trees and other objects that might interfere with the early stage of ascent. And there was always the danger of fire or explosion during the time when the balloon was being readied. A newspaper item of the day read in part: "It is hoped that the spectators may not crowd too near, or interrupt Mr. Blanchard whilst employed in his preparations, as it might be attended with fatal effects, should he be incommoded."[146]

It appears that many of these spectators intended to follow the floating balloon on horseback, attempting to keep apace as best they could. In an open letter to the newspaper, Blanchard explained:

> "You wish to know...where you may order your horses to stand that you may without losing time follow the aerostat. If the day is calm, there will be full time to leave the prison court without precipitation as in that case I shall ascend perpendicularly; but if the wind blows, permit me, gentlemen, to advise you not to attempt following, for the swiftest horses will be unable to keep up with me, especially in a country so intersected with rivers and so covered with woods."[147]

---

146. Blanchard, *op. cit.*, p. 49.

147. *Ibid.*, p. 52.

A short time after Blanchard's first American voyage, he was given permission to construct a rotunda on the Governor's lot on Chestnut Street, where he exhibited the balloon being prepared for his forty-sixth flight. But without the protection of prison walls, the vulnerable aircraft was damaged by stones thrown from the outside.

During this time, in this very city, John Bill Ricketts was conducting a circus on the corner of Twelfth and Market Streets. Here, some time during 1793, Blanchard sent up a balloon with a parachute attached containing a cat and a monkey. Some form of slow ignition was rigged to release the parachute at a certain altitude, which allowed the quadrupeds a safe flotation earthward. A contemporary account relates that the wind was in a southeasterly direction when the balloon left the ground. As it passed over Bush Hill at an altitude of 500 feet the parachute was detached. The balloon then floated in the direction of Gloucester Point and the chute in the direction of Frankford, the future home of John O'Brien's circus enterprises.[148] This ascension at Rickett's Amphitheatre marked the first balloon act with an American circus.

I am indebted to Stuart Thayer for another event concerning an early circus balloon ascension. An announcement in a Nashville, Tennessee paper told of such an occurrence for Messrs. Myers and Johnstone's

---

148. Durang, Charles (partly compiled from the papers of his father, John Durang, with notes by the editors), "The History of the Philadelphia Stage Between the Years 1749 and 1855," serialized in the Philadelphia *Sunday Dispatch*, 1854-1860, Part I, Chapter XXIII, pp. 44-45, microfilm.

benefit with J. Purdy Brown's circus on December 26, 1827. Thayer also sent me an item from the Cincinnati *Daily Enquirer* of 1853 which, although having little to do with this narrative, I cannot resist including it here. On April 24 of that year the paper announced an exhibition called Deihl & Co.'s Hydrogen Menagerie. The animals were all composed of silk cloth inflated with gas and all were somewhat animated and capable of performing tricks. The elephant was twenty-one-feet high and eighteen-feet long. Among other objects, there was a whale some thirty feet in length and a giant twenty-one feet in height, all seemingly representing an early prelude to similar objects used in Macy's annual Christmas parade. In conjunction with this tented attraction was an ascensionist, W. M. Paulin, and fireworks were conducted by Mr. Deihl, advertised as the "celebrated pyrotechnist."[149]

Perhaps the first time a balloon was put to practical use occurred with its introduction by the Union Army early in the Civil War. On June 17, 1861, Thaddeus Lowe, who had recently flown the 900 miles from Cincinnati to Unionville, South Carolina, demonstrated the effectiveness of his soaring vessel to President Lincoln. With his crew, he ascended aloft for a brief period and communicated with the groundlings by telegraph. The performance must have been impressive to the illustrious observers; for, in time, T. S. C. Lowe's Balloon Corps, consisting of a number of free-lance balloonists, was formed to assist the Union

---

149. Cincinnati Daily *Enquirer*, April 24, 1853; May 5, 1853.

Army. Lowe's balloons were put into limited service to aerially observe enemy troop movements and to direct Union artillery. Only a week following his demonstration Lowe and a sketch artist floated a balloon near a Confederate encampment adjacent to Fall's Church, a community near Arlington, Virginia, recording enemy activity for the first time. A month later another of Lowe's ascensionists, John LaMountain, began using balloons for the Federal government at Fort Monroe, near Hampton Roads, Virginia. The forerunner of today's aircraft carrier made an experimental debut on August 3, 1861, when LaMountain launched a balloon from the deck of the ship *Fanny*—which had been especially outfitted for that purpose.

For many of these early balloonists, ascending into the ethers was not simply a dare devil stunt; it was a means of unraveling the science of flight—understanding the effects of air currents, the problems of elevation, the skill of navigation, and the evolution of balloon structure and building materials. But all this was expensive. By his own statement, Blanchard's first American flight, which required "4200 weight of vitriolic acid," which was needed for creating hydrogen, was paid for by his "aerial companions in Europe" at a cost of 100 guineas.[150] And there were, of course, other expenses. The early solution for raising money was through ticket subscriptions. In Blanchard's case, although the entire population of Philadelphia, from 40,000 to 50,000 people, watched the ascension, the

---

150. Blanchard, *op. cit.*, p. 46.

gate receipts totaled a mere $405.[151] The event was observed by nearly the whole of the city from outside the prison walls.

It was ultimately discovered that the sale of tickets was not a feasible means of raising funds. Subsequent aeronauts found it was dangerous to disappoint audiences who had paid their money to see the balloon go up, bad weather being no excuse for cancellation. When a French aeronaut failed to ascend because the wind was close to hurricane level, the Philadelphia citizenry, who had paid to witness the event, broke up his aerial car for souvenirs, shredded his silken balloon, and burned the mansion from which grounds the flight was to have been made. This illustrates the passion of curiosity balloon flights created in the last century. In addition, charging admission did not pay because it was too easy just to save the money and simply remain at a distance to watch. After all, the real enchantment was seeing the craft in the air, not air being pumped into it. Consequently, the best alternative was to find a sponsor to underwrite the exhibition—a civic celebration, agricultural fair, a commercial promotion, etc. With expenses paid for by the sponsoring organization, the ascension became a free act for the purpose of attracting an audience to an event other than solely the aeronautical feat.

Sometime in the 1820s at William Niblo's famous garden in New York City, a Madame Blanchard was "wafted away to the azure vault above town in a

---

151. *Ibid.*, p. 45.

balloon."[152] Niblo's Garden was a fashionable evening resort where ice creams and other delicacies were served and nightly entertainments—musical concerts, rope dancing, pyrotechnic displays and other such diversions—were offered. Was this intrepid lady the wife of Jean Pierre? Or was she an opportunist usurping the Blanchard name? Concurrently to her exhibitions, a man by the name of Robertson was ascending from the grounds of the rival Vauxhall Garden. It was said about that time that "a public garden without a balloon would be as great an anomaly as the theatre without an orchestra."[153] These incidents serve as examples of the direction aeronautic exhibitions had taken—an inducement for public congregation.

The balloon ascension became a daily attraction with circuses in the year following the Civil War. The originator appears to be George W. DeHaven's (1837-1902) show of 1870. The practice began with no fanfare and seemingly no thought of it being innovative. The first reference to it in the New York *Clipper* read: "One of the aeronauts connected with DeHaven's Circus was recently severely injured by falling from the balloon into a summer house at Davenport, Iowa, and his substitute was drowned at Dubuque by falling in the river, we are informed."[154]

DeHaven moved about in Iowa, Illinois and Indiana

---

152. Picton, Col. Tom (edited by William L. Slout), *Old Gotham Theatricals*. San Bernardino, CA: The Borgo Press, 1995.

153. Picton, Col. Tom (edited by William L. Slout), *Fun and Fancy in Old New York*. San Bernardino, CA: The Borgo Press, 1995.

154. New York *Clipper*, June 18, 1870, p. 87.

that season. Then, at the end of July, R. E. J. Miles, a Cincinnati theatrical promoter, purchased the circus, which continued to function under the DeHaven banner. [I venture to remark that DeHaven's managerial history could be likened to a locomotive that halted with frequency to take on fuel.] The company traveled the Ohio River on their boat *Victor* until it reached Wheeling, when they transferred to the Baltimore and Ohio Railroad. At this time it was announced: "A balloon ascension is now made daily in connection with the circus." And a correspondent writing from Camden, South Carolina, where the circus recently had performed, referred to a free balloon ascension prior to the afternoon exhibition.[155]

Balloons for free acts caught on with other circus managers for the 1871 season. Agnes Lake's Hippo-Olympiad was mentioned in the *Clipper* early in January of that year as exhibiting a balloon ascension; but her show may have started the practice in late 1870. By that time, R. E. J. Miles had become managing director for Mrs. Lake, and George W. DeHaven was in advance of the show following the Miles/DeHaven seasonal closing. They apparently carried their propensity for balloon ascensions with them; for at 1:00 P.M. each day, or shortly before the start of Lake's matinee, Prof. J. W. Hayden fired up his equipment and went aloft.[156] The show disbanded for the winter on February 24 at Atlanta, Georgia, and returned to

---

155. New York *Clipper*, August 6, 1870, p. 143; September 3, 1870, p. 175; October 22, 1870, p. 231.

156. New York *Clipper*, January 14, 1871, p. 327.

Cincinnati to prepare for an April re-opening; but not before becoming the second circus to travel with an aeronaut as a free attraction.

G. G. Grady's Old Fashioned Circus began the practice in 1871 also. That is when the circus advertised balloon ascensionist Prof. Terries. This may have been either William or James Terries, both of whom were on the roster as acrobats.[157] Wootten & Haights's Empire City Circus advertised a "Gratuitous Balloon Ascension, Adjoining the Circus Pavilion, at 1 o'clock P.M., prior to the arenic exhibition," with the so-called French aeronaut, Prof. Renno, piloting his monster ball. The ad claimed the circus had eight of these air ships 100 feet high and sixty feet in diameter which allowed them to give daily exhibitions. And finally, James Robinson's Circus, in this same year of 1871, featured the "Celebrated French Aeronaut," Mons. Paul LeGrand.

It appears to me that the early use of balloon ascensions with these companies was, at best, reckless. Unlike the professional flying of such men as Blanchard, Lowe, and LaMountain, the early circus ascensionists do not seem to be skilled aeronauts, but ambitious young men eager to turn a fast dollar, with invented French names and perhaps the added designation of "Professor." Josie DeMott, in the charming book about her life in the circus, characterizes the balloon ascension as "a trick performed by someone with more daring than intelligence." And of the aeronaut, she

---

157. *Ibid.*, p. 11.

writes, "He was always nicknamed Ballooney, usually shortened to Looney."[158] As such, the lives of these men were often shortened as well; or, for the more fortunate, filled with narrow escapes. While in Camilla, Georgia, on January 19, 1871, Lake's balloon caught fire as it began to ascend. The occupant escaped injury by swiftly bailing out at an altitude of a mere thirty-five feet.[159] In Dayton, Ohio on April 21 of that year, just previous to the send-off of G. G. Grady's aeronaut, Terries, who performed on a trapeze bar, the balloon caught fire near its mouth and continued to burn as it rose from the ground. When the air within the bag cooled, the aeronaut descended rapidly but fortunately was able to break the force of his fall by grasping onto a branch of a willow tree. A sprained ankle was his only souvenir.[160] Again in July, when Lake's Hippo-Olympiad was returning from a tour of the West, the Saline County *Journal* of Saline, Kansas, opined:

> "The balloon ascension was not the greatest success in the world. The balloon ascended but Prof. Miles didn't, and thus was our special artist deprived of a visit to the stars. The parachute must have been indisposed, for the balloon seemed to shoot off before there was a good ready. The 'ship of air' turned a complete somersault after going up a few feet, and

---

158. Robinson, Josephine DeMott, *The Circus Lady*, pp. 81-82.
159. New York *Clipper*, February 4, 1871, p. 351.
160. New York *Clipper*, May 6, 1871, p. 39.

caught fire. The fire was speedily extinguished; so was the balloon."[161]

The aeronaut for James Robinson, while exhibiting in Louisville, Kentucky, on July 12, 1871, had a collapse of the balloon which rapidly fell earthward but, fortunately, the craft landed on a rooftop without damage to its passenger.[162] Prof. Fisher of G. G. Grady's circus, who had replaced Terries for a reason to be explained later, was lucky during the Pittsburgh stand on August 3, 1871, when, after attaining some 500 feet of altitude, his balloon suddenly dropped and doused him into the Allegheny River, wherein he swam to a nearby sailboat, safe and uninjured.[163] Again, with James Robinson, in Cincinnati on July 17th, the balloon repeated its erratic behavior, forcing the aeronaut to dive through a friendly second story window of a picture frame factory to safety, which sounds like a spectacular feat in itself. The *Clipper* reporter suggested: "These ascensions with hot air are fool hardy. The man risks his neck every time he goes up."[164] Press agent and circus historian, Charles H. Day, has suggested that Stone & Murray used hot air balloons in the early 1870s but abandoned the scheme on account of the frequent accidents to aeronauts and the

---

161. King, Orin C., "Only Big Show Coming," Part Two, in *Bandwagon*, July-August, 1987, p. 42.

162. New York *Clipper*, July 22, 1871, p. 127.

163. New York *Clipper*, August 12, 1871, p. 151.

164. New York *Clipper*, July 29, 1871, p. 135.

innumerable bills for damages from the descent of the balloon.[165]

These accidents merely delayed the inevitable. A *Clipper* obituary revealed that a Leonardi Torres, who must have been the Terries previously mentioned, a man of about twenty-eight years of age, died on July 22, 1871, making a balloon ascension for G. G. Grady's circus in Massillon, Ohio. While performing aloft on a trapeze, he let loose his grasp to prevent being smothered by the balloon exhaust and fell into the water-filled Ohio Canal, some eight or nine feet deep. Tragically, his feet lodged in the mud at the canal bottom, causing him to drown.[166] Professor Atkins, a twenty year old from Toledo, Ohio, lost his life while with Mike Lipman's circus at Decatur, Alabama, on May 27, 1872. As he was about to go aloft, he remarked apprehensively, "This is the last ascension I'll ever make." And it was. The balloon plummeted into the Tennessee River from a height of about a half-mile and the young man drowned.

Even for skilled acrobats, balloon performing was dangerous and frequently deadly. Washington Harrison Donaldson (1840-1875) was the victim of one of the most famous balloon tragedies. A native Philadelphian and son of an alderman in that city, he was as a child fond of sports and eventually was proficient at balancing on a ladder, walking the tight-rope, etc. Subsequently, he became interested in aeronautics

---

165. Day, Charles H., "History of American Circus and Tented Exhibitions," in *Billboard*, January 5, 1907, p. 20.

166. New York *Clipper*, August 5, 1871, p. 143.

and performing on a trapeze suspended from a balloon. While in Philadelphia, at Broad and Norris Streets, he ascended in a small one-man craft, which became unmanageable and descended near Atco, New Jersey. Three telegrams were sent to Philadelphia, stating that Donaldson had fallen from a great height and been killed, which created quite a sensation, all made plausible by the signature of "J. M. Spencer, M.D." Shortly, other telegrams announced that Donaldson was alive. It later came out that he had sent the telegrams himself and that losing the balloon was a pre-arranged publicity stunt. This came to the attention of P. T. Barnum, who, perhaps out of a feeling of kinship for a fellow "humbugger," hired the young aeronaut.

Donaldson made his last and most famous flight for Barnum's circus in Chicago, when on July 15, 1875, he disappeared over Lake Michigan. After ascending in a tattered balloon used for the free act, he was carried out over the lake and wrecked. Both Donaldson and Greenwood (or Grimwood), a reporter for a Chicago newspaper, were assumed to have perished in the water. The following day, David S. Thomas, the show's press agent, assumed the role of aeronaut and made an ascension himself. It later came out that as an amateur he had previously been involved in some thirty-four trips aloft. The newspaperman's body washed ashore some weeks later, but Donaldson's remains were never recovered.

There were others in the profession, however, on whom Fortune cast a more benevolent spell. Silas M.

Brooks was one. He entered the entertainment business in 1848 when engaged by Barnum to form a Druid band. He manufactured crude horn instruments and grotesque costumes and created a successful act. Later, he organized a circus of his own which featured a balloon ascension. When his aeronaut, a man named Paulin, was taken ill, Brooks donned the aeronaut's garb and completed the scheduled flight. Finding the experience to his liking, he continued in that capacity and accrued a fortune. Where it all went is unexplained, for he died in the poor house in Collinsville, Connecticut, on April 7, 1906.

August Buislay (1847-1911), the most prominent member of the Buislay Family, came to California from France and started a small, one-ring circus. As gymnasts and antipodean artists, the group featured feats of the "Spiral Mountain" and the "Niagara Leap." When the first gas filled balloons came into vogue, August, an intrepid trapeze performer, began making ascensions and ultimately parachuting from the floating air bubble.

Prof. Samuel A. King (1828-1914) was another of the nineteenth-century ascensionists who managed to stay alive in the profession. He was present at the Philadelphia Centennial Exhibition in 1876 and later traveled with Barnum & Bailey. When, during the 1893 World's Columbian Exposition in Chicago, he took a woman passenger aloft, the balloon was blown out over Lake Michigan and both were given up as lost. A revenue cutter was sent to find their remains but before the boat returned the professor landed his craft safely on solid Chicago soil. He lived to die another day, in Philadelphia, from heart failure at the age of 86.[167]

It must here be noted that, whereas the serious aeronauts of the early years had been knowledgeable and precise about their use and preparation of balloons, circuses were far less careful. Instead of using a contemporary system of filling the balloon with hydrogen, they kept to the more primitive and less expensive means of hot air. The inflation process commenced at about a half-hour before send-off when hot air was created by the generation of heat from a temporary furnace built into the ground. When the moment came to ascend, the starter gave the signal and the aeronaut lifted off, usually clinging to a trapeze bar fastened to the balloon. Once aloft, the air voyager was followed on the ground by a man with horse and rig, so that after he alighted he could be swiftly returned to the show lot to relate his perilous journey to the assembled crowd and sell his photographs. With hydrogen, the buoyancy of the balloon could be controlled through careful release of the gas. With hot air, the speed of descent was proportionate to the time it took for the air within the balloon cavity to cool. If conditions were such that it cooled rapidly, the balloon could plummet to the ground at a dangerous pace. This would account for the repeated accidents.

This brings us to the ultimate question: Why did circuses make use of balloon ascensions at this partic-

---

167. Author's notes.

ular time? There is no single answer. A logical one was posed by Bob Parkinson in his 1961 *Bandwagon* article, "Circus Balloon Ascensions." He suggested that the sensational escape from Paris by Leon Gambetta while the city was under siege in October of 1870, during the Franco-Prussian War, which was romanticized through newspaper accounts and illustrated weeklies, influenced circus proprietors to take advantage of the public interest over the event.[168] Still, that does not account for DeHaven's introduction of the balloon ascension, which occurred some months earlier. Certainly the Civil War balloonists contributed a share toward creating public interest, even though they saw limited use and were in operation for only a short period of time.

To me there is a more compelling reason. All of the circuses previously mentioned, the ones using the balloon ascension for a free act during 1870 and 1871, were either rail or boat shows or both. The years from 1850 to 1870 was a period during which there were increased attempts at rail transportation by circuses, as added rail mileage made it easier to fill their dates. Still, these endeavors were not fully successful.

Fred Dahlinger, Jr., in his study of the early railroad circuses, developed some interesting ideas that apply here. He designated the turning point for the railroad circus as being in 1872 when P. T. Barnum's Museum, Menagerie, Caravan and Hippodrome successfully adopted rail travel through a system of loading and

---

168. Parkinson, Bob, "Circus Balloon Ascensions," in *Bandwagon*, March-April, 1961, pp. 4-5.

unloading the wagons from special flat cars and developing a more proficient means of railroad routing. Circuses prior to 1872 loaded onto box cars and generally hired local drays or used a form of "knockdown" wagon to carry the equipment from lot to rail siding, because the enclosed boxcars disallowed the transporting of regular baggage stock. In addition, the railroad system was still not fully developed to efficiently handle show movement. The upshot being, as Dahlinger described it:

> "The circus' inability to exploit rail travel coupled with the railroad system's lack of development caused showmen to downsize their shows to a level which could survive under these restrictive conditions. Virtually everything which was not necessary to house and execute the performance in the big top was eliminated, including the parade, the menagerie and the museum or sideshow. This self-imposed downsizing led to the popular conception that the rail show delivered less for the price of admission than the overland circus."[169]

The balloon ascension at this early stage, then, was a substitute for the parade and menagerie with shows traveling by rail or boat in an attempt to compete with the innumerable wagon shows on the road following the Civil War. As we have mentioned, DeHaven's

---

169. Dahlinger, Fred, Jr., "The Development of the Railroad Circus," Part One, in *Bandwagon*, November-December, 1983, pp. 6-7.

circus moved principally by boat and rail. The others, the Empire City Circus of Wootten and Haight, Lake's Hippo-Olympiad, and James Robinson's Champion Circus all traveled by rail at the time they first adopted the balloon ascension as a free act. According to the *Clipper*, the Empire City Circus "did not make any display," meaning no parade.[170]

During May and June, G. G. Grady's circus traveled by steamer throughout Michigan, ending up at Chicago for the July 4th celebrations. From there they took to the rails for July and August. When Grady gave six exhibitions in Pittsburgh beginning July 31, 1871, a correspondent found the balloon ascension to be the greatest attraction with the company. "This is always a free exhibition and thousands of people witnessed it in Pittsburgh.... Grady didn't take much 'stock' in street parades. His band, mounted on horseback, and a clown in ring costume, also on horseback, constituted the daily procession."[171] Of the James Robinson Circus, the *Clipper* confirmed: "The company travel by rail, so do not pretend to give a gorgeous street procession, but have an outside feature in the shape of a balloon ascension which is connected with the hot air plan."[172] The parade of the Hippo-Olympiad, traveling from the West by rail, was limited to a bandwagon circulating through the streets.[173]

Although the balloon ascension did not supplant the

---

170. New York *Clipper*, May 27, 1871, p. 62.

171. New York *Clipper*, August 12, 1871, p. 151.

172. New York *Clipper*, September 2, 1871, p. 175.

173. King, *op. cit.*, p. 35.

parade or the menagerie or side show, it appears to have been a useful substitute for the managers before the Barnum show opened the door to serious rail travel. And public fascination with circus balloon ascensions existed for another fifty years. The risk to human life was an aspect that made viewing more exciting, an occasional fatality to the aeronaut serving as an added feature to a spectacle that otherwise offered little in the way of variety. Still, the magic of being lifted into the air, defying the law of gravity, moving into what appears to be endless space, is a fulfillment of childhood fantasy. Today the aeronaut has been replaced by the astronaut. The public is still fascinated.

Who can say? Perhaps some day circuses will pitch their tents on Mars.

THE CHICKEN OR THE EGG
A DOUBLE RING CONTROVERSY, PHASE TWO

In an earlier paper, we suggested that P. T. Barnum's Great Traveling World's Fair of 1872 did not originate the two-ring performance as they claimed in their advertising and which had been accepted as factual by later historians. The misinformation was caused by the Barnum show's use of a frequently included line: "The first and only show in the world that uses a double circus ring, and requires a double circus troupe of performers." However, the double-ring referred to the increased space between the ring and the audience, created by the use of a larger canvas pavilion to accommodate an extended seating area. This space, which formed a ring around the ring, was for circuses the origin of what we now refer to as the hippodrome track. Therefore, the true explanation for the advertisements of two rings in 1872 is that there was a new performing area around the single ring that could be used for greater spectacle."[174]

---

174. William L. Slout, "Two Rings and a Hippodrome Track," *Bandwagon*,

This is not to be confused with Franconi's Hippodrome, which exhibited in New York City in 1853, and then went on the road under canvas for two seasons. The Hippodrome used an elongated track within the perimeter of the seating area for races and other sports, but there was no circus ring involved. The space within the oval formed an infield decorated with landscaping. Picking up on the Franconi use, the word "hippodrome" to describe a place of exhibition or form of entertainment appeared occasionally in later circus advertising; but there is nothing to suggest from this that these organizations were anything but a standard one-ring circus.

Further, as we suggested in the previous paper, Barnum show claims for multi-ring performances during the 1873 season were valid. There were two rings and a hippodrome track, and their use was strongly advertised and frequently confirmed in local press stories. For example, the Buffalo *Daily Courier* included this description: "Under the vast Hippodrome Pavilion are three rings, one of which is used entirely for the performances that follow. In the two rings two acts go on simultaneously, but the salient and brilliant features of the act in one ring are so admirably timed with reference to those in the other that confusion is entirely avoided."[175]

From this and other such pieces of information we concluded that P. T. Barnum's Great Traveling World's

---

November-December, 2000.

175. Buffalo (NY) *Daily Courier,* July 2, 1873.

Fair was the first to make use of a double circus ring and that 1873 was the inaugural year.

But wait. There was another organization in contention for that honor: The Great Eastern Menagerie, Museum, Aviary, Circus and Balloon Show, under the management team of Andrew Haight & Co., which made its debut in 1872 out of the remains of the former Col. C. T. Ames' Menagerie, Agnes Lake's Hippo-Olympiad, and Haight's Empire City Circus. The result was a highly successful season, made possible through exaggerated advertising and an aggressively combative policy toward all rivals. In fact, quite clearly, they were intent on forcefully competing with the Barnum show, "copy and conquer."

The Great Eastern was launched at Cincinnati's National Theatre for a week's stay on April 1, 1872. During the summer months it remained in the middle states—Kentucky, Tennessee, Indiana, Illinois, Missouri, Iowa, Minnesota and Wisconsin. There were a few dates in Pennsylvania and New York State in late August before starting south, as it followed a route through Virginia, the Carolinas, Georgia, Florida, Mississippi and Alabama, before winding up at Selma on the 13th of December, after eight months on the road.

Advertised features included the daily balloon ascension; the calliope, the only one on the road that year; the elephant Bismarck; four immense pavilions; and "twelve shows in one." However, when St. Louis was advertised for five days beginning July 22, we see for the first time the claim of "The Six Great Tent

Show," not four as had previously been claimed. The ads also read, "DOUBLE CIRCUS RING. Two performances in separate pavilions at the same time, by the first talent of Europe and America." Is it possible when at this St. Louis stand the Great Eastern became the first two-ring American circus?

Following the Great Eastern's opening, the St. Louis *Democrat* favorably reported that a large crowd had filled the street, "attracted by the gorgeous parade which was enlivened by three bands of music, a steam calliope, a cloud of banners, squadrons of prancing horses, and a number of wild beasts." The opening night audience was "almost uncontrollably large," according to the paper. "It surged back and forward like a great sea, rippling waves against the walls of tents, coursing irresistibly through the passage ways that connected the different apartments and drifting about in the wide hippodromes." The writer was pleased with the selection of the performers, which was confirmed by "the constant storms of applause."[176]

The *Democrat* of the 26th gave a final note in summary of the week's stay.

> "The exhibitions have been alike profitable to the public and to the managers, the latter having reaped a harvest from the immense throngs that have been constantly in attendance. Among the many attractions during the week have been the performances of Miss Emma Lake, who has a very winning face and

---

176. St. Louis (MO) *Democrat*, July 23, 1872.

is an exceedingly graceful and dashing equestrienne."

However, not once did the items in the local newspapers mention two rings in separate tents giving simultaneous performances. What, then, is the explanation? The Great Eastern's chief rival, the Barnum show, was using the phrase "Six Separate Colossal Tents" this year and, as we have stated, had frequently included in its advertising: "The first and only show in the world that uses a double circus ring, and requires a double circus troupe of performers."

Therefore, our explanation for the Great Eastern claims is that, because the Barnum show followed the Great Eastern into St. Louis by a week, the Great Eastern usurped the Barnum advertisements by claiming six tents and a second ring of its own. It is true that occasionally during the remainder of the season the Great Eastern laid claims to performances in two rings within its display ads; but no local papers we surveyed referred to such an occurrence. This includes such journals as the New York *Clipper*, the Cleveland *Herald*, the Pittsburgh *Post*, the Charleston *Daily Courier*, the Augusta *Daily Chronicle*, the Savannah *Morning News*, the Mobile *Daily Register* and the Atlanta *Constitution*. We can only conclude that neither the Barnum show nor the Great Eastern used two rings for the season of 1872.

Yet, there is conflicting evidence we cannot adequately explain. There are two men connected with the Great Eastern in 1872 who have written briefly of their experience—George W. Hall, Jr. and John A. Dingess. Hall's article in the *Billboard* of June 24, 1922, includes absolutely nothing about a double ring, but Dingess, who was an agent for the Great Eastern during the latter part of the 1872 season, wrote in his unpublished manuscript that DeHaven conceived the idea of the second ring. "Not two rings, wherein inferior performances were given, as is the custom nowadays, but two separate tents, with equestrian performances in each, at one and the same time."[177] Unfortunately, that is the extent of his explanation. How could this have been accomplished? Two performances occurring in separate tents at the same time, with competing noises of band and audience? In addition, how was it done with a performing roster that was seemingly the same as at the start of the season?

During this period, many people, for whom circus performances were anathema, paid their ticket and visited only the menagerie, justifying that exhibition as educational. Could it be that the Great Eastern menagerie remained open while the arenic program was going on and that some sort of display or performing exhibition with its animals occurred? Alternatively, could it be that the side show was in constant rotation throughout the evening? This represents mere speculation as we search for an answer to conflicting information.

However, the Great Eastern did make use of a double-

---

177. Dingess includes a reproduction of an ad from a Pensacola, Florida, paper dated October 19, 1872, and ending with the customary identification, "John A. Dingess, agent."

ring during the 1873 season. Let us take a look. With the election over, Ulysses S. Grant winning handily, the proprietors of the Great Eastern entered a new year with money in their pockets; but the management team parted ways following the successful first season, with George W. DeHaven and R. E. J. Miles joining Spencer Q. Stokes in taking out the Great Chicago Show.[178]

The early listing in the *Clipper* designated the Great Eastern's management as Haight & Co., indicating one or more others had an interest in the show. James S. Totten, the treasurer, is one possibility. We can report, using the Great Eastern's sixteen-page 1873 Advance Herald as a source, that the concern was operated by Andrew Haight, general director; Jacob Haight, financial manager; Ben Maginley, manager; A. H. Penny, assistant manager; W. W. Durand, general agent; George Guilford, press agent; J. S. Totten, treasurer; J. L. Breese and Ben S. Potter, ticket agents; Col. Judd Webb, master of canvas; W. B. Carroll, equestrian director; H. J. Leech, contracting agent; Charles Sivalls, advertising agent; John Johnson, animal superintendent; W. D. Storey and Jacob Muller, band leaders; Frank Moore and W. Scott, program agents;

---

178. At the opening of the season, Stokes was listed as sole proprietor of the Great Chicago. DeHaven was general manager and Miles the business manager and treasurer; but the latter two must have had an interest in the concern at the outset as well. From the *Clipper*'s listing, the wagon show carried twelve tents—one 150 feet by 200 feet, one 100-foot round, and ten 80-foot rounds; sixteen cages, a small museum, and a sixteen piece orchestra. The arenic performance was built around the great James Robinson, supported by the Stokes family, the Royal Yedo Japanese Troupe, twenty-four children riders, William Gorman, clowns Sam Stickney, William Burke, etc. There would be a rocky road ahead.

Dan Monahan, master of horse.[179]

It was announced in the early *Clipper* that the show was to travel by rail using sixty-two cars. A later count by an Indianapolis reporter was fifty-four. According to him, there were two sleeping coaches for the actors, three box cars for the working men, two for "canvassers," one for patent gas, one for properties, one for wardrobe, one for museum and refreshments, nine for the horses, and the remaining for the animals. There were two cages to a flat. The elephants were chained to a ringbolt fastened to the floor of the car. Both elephants and camels were required to get down on their knees to enter and leave the car.[180]

Still quoting from the *Clipper*, the street parade would display forty-one dens, twenty women on horseback, a steam calliope, three full brass and reed bands and a martial band. There was to be twelve tents using three separate entrances; and, as in 1872, a double circus performance in separate pavilions. Haight & Co. shared the privileges, for the most part with men already serving in other positions. Ben Maginley and Pete Gannen had the concert; W. W. Durand and J. L. Breese, the candy stands inside and outside; and Pat Harris, the sideshow. Herr Elijah Lengel was replaced this year by Agnes Lake, who performed as Mlle. Eugenie DeLorme; but was supported by H. Saunders, supposedly an English animal tamer. The stunt of having the various cats "loose" atop a parade wagon

---

179. *Great Eastern Advance Herald*, 1873.

180. Indianapolis (IN) *Sentinel*, April 10, 1873.

was continued from the 1872 season.[181]

The performing roster, many repeats from the previous year, included Emma Lake, the Carrolls—Master Willie, Marie, Annie, W. B. and Dolly Varden—C. H. Lowry, Fred Sylvester, Mlle. Ben Soiti, Adolph Barrabo, riders; Miaco Brothers, Jerome Tuttle, Tom Watson, W. Carroll, T. V. Ashton, A. P. Durand, W. Painter, W. Carr, A. Penny, F. Moore, Adolph Barrabo, Master George and Eddie, gymnasts; Ben Maginley, C. Lee Fowler, Al Miaco, clowns; John Williams, elephant performer.[182] The Advance Herald carried the additional names of Willis Cobb and his trained dogs; the Davenport Brothers, posturers, contortionists and tumblers; Charles Spencer, acrobat and gymnast; J. C. Long, Herculean performer; Shappe & Whitney, trapeze artists; and Sam McFlynn, clown.

The claims that were broadcast were similar to those of the previous year. The Advance Herald went all out with: "$100,000 Challenge," "Only Twelve Show Tent on Earth," "Twelve Center-Pole Show," "Double Circus Company," "Grand Street Pageant and Processions Over Two Miles Long," "Four Separate Trains Numbering 100 Cars," "20 Beautiful Young Lady Riders," "Over 2,000 Men and Horses," "A Colossal Aggregation, Reorganized and Equipped Especially for the Season of 1873."

Indeed, the company was reorganized and enlarged from the previous year. That the features of the 1872

---

181. New York *Clipper* supplement, April 19, 1873.
182. *Ibid.*

show were grossly overstated in their advertising was confirmed in the 1873 *Advance Herald*.

> "And now, kind reader, you will say we promise much, and that 'so-and-so' has 'humbugged' you in the past. We grant it; and submit to you a proposition, which, if entertained, will protect you from deception in the future. Go to our different places of appointment. Look at our procession; count the dens, the horses—and behold the tigers, lions, leopards, elephants, camels, etc., unchained and 'loose in the streets.' Listen to the weird and bewitching music of the mammoth steam piano, drawn by dancing teams of dapple steeds. Go to the ground where pavilions are stretched like winged things of life before you, and count them; and if you do not find everything just as we represent it, turn away and go home without patronizing us. Always judge exhibitions by this never-failing standard and you will not be deceived."

One wonders how many patrons were willing to suspend their disbelief on reading the above, as the 1873 advertising continued to make exaggerated assertions far in excess of reality.

The salaries of the performers were included in the text of the Advance Herald, which we are quick to note, may or may not be factual. At the very least, however, they indicate the ranking within the company. Miss Emma Lake, received $250 per week; Mlle. Marie Elise, $300; W. B. Carroll and family, five in number—La Petite Annie, Masters Willie and Dolly Varden, and Mme. and W. B. Carroll—$350; Charles H. Lowry, $125; Alfred, William and Jerome Miaco, $250; Adolph Barrabo, $80; Tom Watson, $60; Fred Sylvester, $100; Jerome Tuttle, Batchelor, Norris, Storey, Wallace, Williams, Esler, and others, from $25 to $50; Mlle. Eugenie De Lorme (Agnes Lake), $140.

There was a dubious beginning for the Haight organization's new season. The intention was to open in Louisville, Kentucky, on March 10 in the Exposition Building; but on the 8th an injunction was issued on behalf of James E. Cooper to prevent any circus company from performing there until Cooper's circus, which had been wintering in the building, ended its occupancy following its opening on the 31st. This forced the Great Eastern to move under canvas. All went well for the March 10 matinee, a packed house, no less. However, the evening performance was interrupted by a gale that came up around 10 P.M., snapping the centerpole in two, breaking ropes loose from the ground and collapsing the entire spread of the main canvas on top of the spectators. Pandemonium ensued, with women fainting, children screaming, and the caged animals in a nearby tent creating a spine-chilling racket. The management acted promptly in extricating the mass of humanity from beneath the flattened tent. At least two people died and untold numbers were injured, but the efforts of the circus men limited what could have been a far greater disaster. The tent was restored and re-erected the following day and no performances were lost. Haight wisely offered the entire receipts of the matinee to the sufferers.

The circus went indoors for the Cincinnati stand, four days beginning March 26, at the Rink on Freeman and Laurel Streets, with two performances daily. The *Times* responded with the following assessment:

> "The grand zoological and arenic combination, now in the fullest tide of popular favor, had immense bonuses yesterday afternoon and last night at the rink. It is estimated that over five thousand people were turned from the doors last night, unable to gain admission. This will not be wondered at when the perfection of the exhibition is remembered. No show of its kind for years has taken such hold of public favor, and none has received so liberal patronage. The animal collection is very fine, embracing many rare and heretofore unseen specimens, besides a complete list of the domestic species. The circus part of the entertainment is certainly *au fait*, and equestriennes, riders, posturers, tumblers, acrobats, and gymnasts each deserve special mention."[183]

No mention was made of a double-ring performance.

The Great Eastern spent April and May in Ohio,

---

183. Cincinnati (OH) *Times*, as repeated in the Keokuk (IA) *Daily Gate City*, April 16, 1873.

Indiana, Illinois and Michigan. There was competition early in the tour at Belleville, Illinois, and Evansville, Indiana, with another circus that sported an even longer title—the Great Trans-Atlantic Exposition, Museum, Aviary, Aquarium, Polytechnic Institute, Menagerie and Circus. The proprietors were P. A. Older and J. M. Chandler. The Great Eastern appeared at Evansville on April 12, the Trans-Atlantic arrived ahead on the 4th; the Trans-Atlantic was at Belleville on the 9th, the Great Eastern on April 14. Not unexpectedly, Older and Chandler equaled Haight & Co. in exaggerated claims of size and excellence. "Largest Show in the World!" "12 Mammoth Tents." Not to mention a museum that contained 100,000 curiosities, the only white elephant on exhibition, a monster black rhinoceros, and a troupe of 100 performers. Like the Great Eastern, the rival advertised a daily balloon ascension and, astonishingly, two rings with performances in each at the same time.

We have no record of how the two shows fared at Evansville and Belleville; certainly, the Great Eastern had the stronger company. We mention the confrontation to show how occasionally Haight and associates received a taste of their own medicine.

The Great Eastern spent a week in St. Louis beginning April 15 on a lot between Eleventh and Twelfth Streets, opposite Four Courts, where more accolades were handed out. "No institution of its character has achieved more deserved popularity in this city than the really colossal Great Eastern, and, considering the very unpropitious state of the weather the last three days, none have received a more liberal patronage. Perfect in all its several departments, elegant in all its appointments, and elaborate in every detail, it justly and properly ranks among the first mammoth combinations of the entire world....The circus part of the entertainment comprises the *crème de la crème* of the circle."[184] Still no indication of a double ring.

The circus missed a performance at Indianapolis on April 9, arriving too late for the evening show. An accident along the route from Connersville was the cause of the delay. About 6 A.M. the train pulled into Union Station, and then continued on to the vicinity of the old circus grounds at West Georgia Street. Performances were given there the following day. "Ben Maginley, the veteran circus manager, is in charge of the establishment this season," the *Journal* of the 10th read, "and his name is guaranty that everything is the best of its kind to be had."

Keokuk, Iowa, was visited a full month ahead of the Trans-Atlantic. The *Daily Gate City* reported good attendance at the circus on April 21, in spite of the questionable spring weather and bad roads.

> "Since its appearance here last year the Great Eastern's proportions have been largely augmented and it is now one of the most gigantic institutions ever organized in this country. The street procession yesterday morning surpassed anything of the kind ever seen in Keokuk....

---

184. St. Louis (MO) *Daily Globe*, April 17, 1873.

The Great Eastern is a modern triumph in the show line, and is entitled to a position in the very front ranks of the big institutions of the present day."[185]

What about a double-ring?

From a stop at Peoria on April 28, a *Clipper* correspondent estimated that the spread of canvas was greater and covered more ground than any previous circus that had visited the city. The twelve tents were lighted by self-generating gas. The street parade had one martial and two brass bands, all under the leadership of Prof. W. D. Storey. The performance orchestra numbered twenty-five. The menagerie had forty-four cages. A side show consisted of a Punch and Judy, two cages of animals, an albino boy, a four-footed child and magician Prof. Collier. Ring stand-outs worthy of mention by our writer were Charles Lee Fowler, "one of the most perfect we have ever seen in the ring, his jokes and gags are new, and done with a nicety that at once commands the respect and applause of all;" fellow clown, Sam McFlynn, "also a very clever performer, and with more experience will make a first-rate artist;" and "Dolly Varden, son of Mr. W. B. Carroll, and to all appearances three years old" (Varden was Carroll's ward, not his son, and was a dwarf, not an infant).[186] However, there was nothing so far to confirm a double-ring performance.

Competition was heating up in May, which included

---
185. Keokuk (IA) *Daily Gate City*, April 22, 1873.

186. New York *Clippe*r, May 10, 1873.

an altercation between the Great Eastern's man, Atkinson, and Robert Dingess, agent for Forepaugh, at the St. Joseph Hotel in South Bend, Indiana. Bitter words between them reportedly led to Dingess being struck by Atkinson, who then pulled out a revolver. Bystanders quickly interfered, after which the Great Eastern representative was whisked off to jail. Bail was set at $500. But with Dingess fleeing town on an early morning train, Atkinson was released.

The circus moved into Michigan for several dates. At Jackson on the 13th, the *Daily Citizen* writer established his proficiency in arithmetic. We include it in its entirety because of its unvarnished view of the goings-on.

> "For many days the populace of central Michigan have waited for the event of what was advertised as 'The Great Eastern Menagerie, Museum, Aviary, Circus, Roman Hippodrome, Egyptian Caravan and Balloon Show.' The huge advertisement in the newspapers and the large bills explaining the magnificence of the concern served to call out quite a large number of people. It was proclaimed that 100 railroad cars and four locomotives were used to transport this show, which was termed 'A Giant Among Its Fellows.' The populace was a little taken back when they saw forty-one cars brought the Great Eastern to town. The street procession was stated to be two miles long, composed of cages, 100 horsemen, four

bands, etc. The male and female persons on horseback numbered twenty people, with twenty-six cages and wagons, one small elephant, whose blanket had the gilded name of 'Conqueror' inscribed thereon. There were three bands, the first composed of eight pieces, the next of eight pieces, and the martial band of six pieces. There were two camels in the procession, and one cage had a tiger and a couple of panthers on the roof. After the procession had peregrinated through the streets, the people went to look for the twelve tents. They could discover but four tents and a sideshow tent. No one could find the forty-one dens of wild beasts, but there were eighteen, filled with birds, monkeys, lions and a few rare animals. We looked all over for the breathing sea monster, but he had ceased to breathe and was out of sight. The 'steam piano' brought up the rear of the procession, but it provoked merriment instead of wonder. It was not visible after the parade. It was quite a burlesque in its line, and should be kept out of sight after being once seen. The great museum could not be found, without it was a sideshow of small dimensions. The forty-four feet of snakes were not seen, and the menagerie did not contain a quarter of the animals advertised. The 'Aviary' had dried up and didn't bloom here. The circus performance was very good, and a redeeming feature of the whole 'Great Eastern.' The two rings were a novelty. The people had been led to expect a leviathan concern, but the show does not possess many more attractions than less pretentious organizations. It received a liberal patronage, but did not satisfy the people, whose expectations had been wrought up to the highest pitch by the great announcements. In fact, a great many people went home with the thought that they had been considerably humbugged and thought the 'Great Eastern' was a fraud in many points. The thousands who had come to town were disappointed and chagrined. If the show had made less pretensions, and less claim to being a monster organization, it would not have been so bad, but people were led to believe that it would be the biggest thing that ever came here, and in this they were much disappointed. They would have been content if the half promised had been carried out, but it was not. The 'Great Eastern' will have to add much to its attractions, before it can come up to its pretensions."[187]

Ah-hah! "The two rings were a novelty."

More squabbles occurred on May 26 at Detroit. Letters had appeared in the press, supposedly from citizens, condemning the Great Eastern as an imposter. W. W. Durand took umbrage at the inserts and sued Barnum's agent, William McLaughlin, and Forepaugh's

---

187. Jackson (MI) *Daily Citizen*, May 14, 1873.

agent, John Dingess, for libel; and the two men were consigned to the lockup. McLaughlin was released on the 28th; Dingess experienced a longer confinement. In retaliation, the latter man charged Jacob Haight with libel and had him arrested. J. M. French and Fred B. Hooper put up security for Haight and he was released.

Most of June was occupied in Canada and New York state.[188] Buffalo was visited for two days, June 12 and 13, setting up on a Main Street lot, between Tupper and Goodell. The procession drew a large crowd; after which, Prof. Reno ascended in his balloon inflated with air from an alcohol fire. The afternoon performance was well attended and at night, "the very large canvas was packed to the utmost capacity." The man from the *Courier* complimented the management for the smooth and rapid change from one act to another, and found the carrying act of W. B. Carroll and his boy, Dolly Varden, praiseworthy.[189]

Advertisements for Buffalo promised "two sets of performers, giving double acts in separate rings under one canvas at the same time." In a post-appearance item, the *Courier* confirmed this with "the arena is divided into two rings, in which two separate performances go on simultaneously, so that the audience is kept on alert from beginning to end."[190]

July and August were spent in New Jersey and

---

188. While in London, Ontario, Ben Maginley received word of the death of his little daughter in Lansing, MI, for which he immediately left.

189. Buffalo (NY) *Courier*, June 13, 1873, reprinted in the Ft. Scott (KS) *Daily Monitor*, March 25, 1874.

190. *Ibid.*

Pennsylvania. The date at Easton, Pennsylvania, on July 22 prompted the *Daily Express* to include a eulogy to Mlle Marie Elise (Marie Carroll, adopted daughter of Barney Carroll).

> "An Artiste.—Mlle. Marie Elise, the leading equestrienne of the Great Eastern Consolidation, fully bears out her reputation as one of the best lady riders in the country. Her skill, style and graceful horsewomanship proclaim her 'to the manner born,' and that a life spent in the ring will win honor and fame for the hard-working and accomplished artiste. Her feats, however difficult, are easily and beautifully done, and many of them appear simple from the easy grace from which they are performed. One of Mlle's most noted acts is leaping through a hoop so small that it will scarcely pass over her skirts and from the back of a horse in rapid motion. She has certainly reached a high point in her profession, and may feel that she has well earned her laurels."[191]

The circus arrived at the commons near the Lancaster Manufacturing Company's works on Sunday, August 24, where it was greeted with a crowd of about a thousand bystanders to witness the set up. The following day, circus day, the number increased by four or five thousand. The Lancaster *Daily Evening Express* acknowledged the balloon ascension to be the best

---

191. Reprinted in the New York *Clipper*, August 30, 1873.

feature of the event, performed by "an intrepid young aeronaut, a mere boy," who landed safely at some point behind the Wetzel farm near the county hospital. The paper also reported the presence of a number of pickpockets, who were apparently operating with some success and perhaps immunity.

In the evening, shortly before the ring performance began, the canvas caught fire, ignited by sparks from the steam calliope. "There was no water at hand, but plenty of lemonade, and 'circus lemonade' being the nearest approach to muddy water that we know of, we cannot deplore its use for putting out the flames." Thereby, a catastrophe was averted, leaving the damage to a mere hole some seven feet in diameter.

> "Altogether, we do not know that the circus benefited us much as a community. We are certain of one thing—it took between $2,000 and $3,000 of the hard earnings of our middle and poorer classes out of the city, leaving nothing in exchange but the recollections of a heated tent, tame equestrianism, stale and vulgar jokes, and on many instances sore heads and terribly depleted pocket books—if indeed the pocket book was permitted to remain at all."[192]

The circus started south in September. An accident occurred on the 7th while the two show trains were en route from Westminster to Baltimore on the Western Maryland Railroad. A landslide caused two of the

---

192. (Lancaster PA) *Daily Evening Express*, August 26, 1873.

cars—one a sleeper and passenger car, the other a freight car—to jump the track. The latter, containing the small elephant, a camel and a buffalo, turned over. The animals were not hurt and three of the passengers were only slightly injured. After being delayed four hours, the trains arrived at their destination.

The *American and Commercial Advertiser* greeted the first day of Baltimore's three-day stand—September 8, 9, 10—with satisfaction; "There was an immense throng at the circus last night, but the accommodations of the mammoth pavilion are so excellent that all were comfortably seated. Everything was on a colossal scale.... The menagerie is divided into three sections, each of which occupies a pavilion. By this arrangement the animals can be seen at leisure, and there is never so great a crowd around the cages as to obstruct the view." The trained horses and the trapeze performers attracted special attention from the writer.[193]

Washington, D.C. was visited on the 12th and 13th to large attendance, where Gen. W. T. Sherman and family enjoyed the second night performance. A correspondent reported that two ring performances were given simultaneously. The trapeze act of Shappee, Whitney and the Miaco Brothers, the feats of horsemanship by the Carroll children, and the trained horses presented by Emma Lake and W. B. Carroll were considered the features of the show.[194]

The *Republican* reported that W. W. Durand

---

193. Baltimore (MD) *American and Commercial Advertiser*, September 9, 1873.

194. New York *Clipper*, September 20, 1873.

(now called Major Durand, having served in the Confederate army) was presented some weeks prior to the show's arrival with a gift from his colleagues, a set of gold studs, sleeve and collar buttons, as a mark of esteem. They were manufactured by Galt Brothers of Washington, and cost $80.

Richmond was a battleground. There was an encounter with L. B. Lent's New York Circus in Lent's first southern tour under that name. The Great Eastern preceded the New York Circus by showing on September 24 and 25 on the corner of Second and Leigh Streets, ahead of Lent's, which set up on the same lot for the 29th and 30th. At Raleigh, North Carolina, where the Great Eastern performed in Baptist Grove on October 3, the New York Circus arrived a week later on the 10th with the usual "Wait for the Big Show," and stole the Barnum thunder with the proclamation: "Greatest Show on Earth." Lack of newspaper reaction leaves us in the dark as to who was the winner on either occasion.

Three performances were advertised for the August, Georgia, stand on October 27, at 10 A.M., 2 P.M. and 7 P.M. The *Daily Chronicle and Sentinel* proclaimed that the stretch of canvas was the largest ever seen before. It was literally packed on opening night. "The performance took place in two rings and was excellent in every particular. The bareback riding was especially fine, and we do not think can be surpassed. The trained horses are among the best that have ever been brought to this city." At the evening performance, Major W. W.

Durand again was called forth and presented with a gift, this time a gold watch and chain and gold-headed cane, purchased at the local establishment of F. A. Braho & Co. The newspaper also lauded the proficiency of the man behind the ticket window.

> "Among the many wonders of the Great Eastern is one not mentioned on the bills, but a feature nevertheless, most noticeable. Mr. George W. Zebold, properly termed the champion ticket seller, was the observed of all observers last night upon the Parade Ground. The readiness with which he handles the currency is not only remarkable, but also astonishing. It matters not what the denomination—a one, a five, ten, twenty or fifty—there's your ticket and your change, quick as thought, round and correct. The way the bank folks look upon Mr. Zebold would indicate that he might profitably change his business."[195]

Two days in Atlanta—December 2 and 3—at the site of the Georgia Western Railroad depot on Marietta Street, closed the season. The *Constitution* noted that the opening night attendance was "witnessed by the largest concourse of people we ever saw under canvas in this city." Furthermore, "the immensity of the exhibition and the variety of entertainments seemed to be an agreeable surprise to everybody, and we heard no

---

195. New York *Clipper*, September 20, 1873.

word spoken save of praise and commendation."[196] The Great Eastern had survived the great Panic of 1873.

In summary, as we have shown, the Great Eastern made use of a double-ring during the 1873 season. However, no local confirmation of its use prior to the month of May was found, leaving us to speculate it was added two months into the season as an emulation of the Barnum show, bolstering the Great Eastern claim of "Double Circus Company" and "A Colossal Aggregation, Reorganized and Equipped Especially for the Season of 1873." We found no indication of a double-ring in April appearances at Louisville, Cincinnati, St. Louis, Indianapolis and Keokuk, Iowa. The first real acknowledgement came from an account in the Jackson, Michigan, *Daily Citizen* of May 14 with: "The two rings were a novelty." In June, advertisements for Buffalo promised "two sets of performers, giving double acts in separated rings under one canvas at the same time." In a post-appearance item, the Buffalo *Courier* verified this with "the arena is divided into two rings, in which two separate performances go on simultaneously, so that the audience is kept on alert from beginning to end." But once the second ring was added, it appears to have been used throughout the remainder of the season. For example, the *American and Commercial Advertiser* greeted the first day of Baltimore's three-day stand—September 8, 9, 10—with: "There are two rings; both in full view of the whole audience, and the performance in

---

196. Atlanta (GA) *Constitution*, December 3, 1873.

each one would constitute a splendid exhibit in itself." Washington, D.C. followed on September 12 and 13, where a *Clipper* correspondent, writing on the 14th, stated: "In the circus pavilion two ring performances are given simultaneously." An advertisement for an appearance of the circus at Charleston, South Carolina, for October 20 included "Every act doubles in two rings at the same hour under one grand pavilion." The Augusta, Georgia, *Daily Chronicle and Sentinel* of October 28 reported: "The performance took place in two rings and was excellent in every particular."

Both the Barnum show and the Great Eastern originated double-ring performances for the season of 1873, one or the other being the first to offer them, if only by the "length of a nose." The Great Eastern opened the season at Louisville on March 10. The Barnum show opened at the former Empire rink in New York City, now called the American Institute, on March 29 for two weeks, half a month later than the Great Eastern, and from a description in the New York Times of April 4, we know there were performances in two rings simultaneously. Consequently, until better information is uncovered, we have to congratulate the Greatest Show on Earth for being the first to exhibit as a double-ring circus.

ABOUT THE AUTHOR

WILLIAM L. SLOUT, an Emeritus Professor at California State University, San Bernardino, has written or edited a score of books on theatre and circus history, many of them published by the Borgo Press imprint of Wildside Press. He lives and works in Southern California.

www.ingramcontent.com/pod-product-compliance
Lightning Source LLC
LaVergne TN
LVHW041617070426
835507LV00008B/303